Kaplan Publishing are constantly finding new ways to make a difference to your studies and our exciting online resources really do offer something different to students look~~ing for exam success~~

This book comes with free MyKaplan onlin~~e~~ ... an study anytime, anywhere. **This free onlin~~e~~ ... separately and is included in the price o~~f the book.~~**

I0587783

Having purchased this book, you have access to the following online study materials:

CONTENT	AAT	
	Text	Kit
Electronic version of the book	✓	✓
Progress tests with instant answers	✓	
Mock assessments online	✓	✓
Material updates	✓	✓

How to access your online resources

Kaplan Financial students will already have a MyKaplan account and these extra resources will be available to you online. You do not need to register again, as this process was completed when you enrolled. If you are having problems accessing online materials, please ask your course administrator.

If you are not studying with Kaplan and did not purchase your book via a Kaplan website, to unlock your extra online resources please go to www.mykaplan.co.uk/addabook (even if you have set up an account and registered books previously). You will then need to enter the ISBN number (on the title page and back cover) and the unique pass key number contained in the scratch panel below to gain access. You will also be required to enter additional information during this process to set up or confirm your account details.

If you purchased through the Kaplan Publishing website you will automatically receive an e-mail invitation to MyKaplan. Please register your details using this email to gain access to your content. If you do not receive the e-mail or book content, please contact Kaplan Publishing

Your Code and Information

This code can only be used once for the registration of one book online. This registration and your online content will expire when the final sittings for the examinations covered by this book have taken place. Please allow one hour from the time you submit your book details for us to process your request.

Please scratch the film to access your unique code.

Please be aware that this code is case-sensitive and you will need to include the dashes within the passcode, but not when entering the ISBN.

KAPLAN

PUBLISHING

AAT

AQ2016

Bookkeeping Transactions

EXAM KIT

This Exam Kit supports study for the following AAT qualifications:
AAT Foundation Certificate in Accounting – Level 2
AAT Foundation Diploma in Accounting and Business – Level 2
AAT Foundation Certificate in Bookkeeping – Level 2
AAT Foundation Award in Accounting Software – Level 2
AAT Level 2 Award in Accounting Skills to Run Your Business
AAT Foundation Certificate in Accounting at SCQF Level 5

British Library Cataloguing-in-Publication Data

A catalogue record for this book is available from the British Library.

Published by:

Kaplan Publishing UK

Unit 2 The Business Centre

Molly Millar's Lane

Wokingham

Berkshire

RG41 2QZ

ISBN: 978-1-78740-794-7

© Kaplan Financial Limited, 2020

Printed and bound in Great Britain.

CONTENTS

Features in this exam kit

In addition to providing a wide ranging bank of real exam style questions, we have also included in this kit:

- unit-specific information and advice on exam technique

- our recommended approach to make your revision for this particular unit as effective as possible.

You will find a wealth of other resources to help you with your studies on the AAT website:

www.aat.org.uk/

Quality and accuracy are of the utmost importance to us so if you spot an error in any of our products, please send an email to mykaplanreporting@kaplan.com with full details, or follow the link to the feedback form in MyKaplan.

Our Quality Co-ordinator will work with our technical team to verify the error and take action to ensure it is corrected in future editions.

UNIT-SPECIFIC INFORMATION

THE EXAM

FORMAT OF THE ASSESSMENT

The assessment will comprise ten independent tasks. Students will be assessed by computer-based assessment.

In any one assessment, students may not be assessed on all content, or on the full depth or breadth of a piece of content. The content assessed may change over time to ensure validity of assessment, but all assessment criteria will be tested over time.

The learning outcomes for this unit are as follows:

	Learning outcome	Weighting
1	Understand financial transactions within a bookkeeping system	10%
2	Process customer transactions	10%
3	Process supplier transactions	15%
4	Process receipts and payments	25%
5	Process transactions through the ledgers to the trial balance	40%
	Total	**100%**

Time allowed

1 hour and 30 minutes.

PASS MARK

The pass mark for all AAT CBAs is 70%.

 Always keep your eye on the clock and make sure you attempt all questions!

DETAILED SYLLABUS

The detailed syllabus and study guide written by the AAT can be found at:

www.aat.org.uk/

INDEX TO QUESTIONS AND ANSWERS

EXAM TECHNIQUE

- **Do not skip any of the material** in the syllabus.

- **Read each question** *very* carefully.

- **Double-check your answer** before committing yourself to it.

- Answer **every** question – if you do not know an answer to a multiple choice question or true/false question, you don't lose anything by guessing. Think carefully before you **guess**.

- If you are answering a multiple-choice question, **eliminate first those answers that you know are wrong.** Then choose the most appropriate answer from those that are left.

- **Don't panic** if you realise you've answered a question incorrectly. Getting one question wrong will not mean the difference between passing and failing.

Computer-based exams – tips

- Do not attempt a CBA until you have **completed all study material** relating to it.

- On the AAT website there is a CBA demonstration. It is **ESSENTIAL** that you attempt this before your real CBA. You will become familiar with how to move around the CBA screens and the way that questions are formatted, increasing your confidence and speed in the actual exam.

- Be sure you understand how to use the **software** before you start the exam. If in doubt, ask the assessment centre staff to explain it to you.

- Questions are **displayed on the screen** and answers are entered using keyboard and mouse. At the end of the exam, you are given a certificate showing the result you have achieved.

- In addition to the traditional multiple-choice question type, CBAs will also contain **other types of questions**, such as number entry questions, drag and drop, true/false, pick lists or drop down menus or hybrids of these.

- In some CBAs you will have to type in complete computations or written answers.

- You need to be sure you **know how to answer questions** of this type before you sit the exam, through practice.

KAPLAN PUBLISHING

KAPLAN'S RECOMMENDED APPROACH

QUESTION PRACTICE IS THE KEY TO SUCCESS

Success in professional examinations relies upon you acquiring a firm grasp of the required knowledge at the tuition phase. In order to be able to do the questions, knowledge is essential.

However, the difference between success and failure often hinges on your exam technique on the day and making the most of the revision phase of your studies.

The **Kaplan Study Text** is the starting point, designed to provide the underpinning knowledge to tackle all questions. However, in the revision phase, poring over text books is not the answer.

Kaplan Pocket Notes are designed to help you quickly revise a topic area; however you then need to practise questions. There is a need to progress to exam style questions as soon as possible, and to tie your exam technique and technical knowledge together.

The importance of question practice cannot be over-emphasised.

The recommended approach below is designed by expert tutors in the field, in conjunction with their knowledge of the examiner and the specimen assessment.

You need to practise as many questions as possible in the time you have left.

OUR AIM

Our aim is to get you to the stage where you can attempt exam questions confidently, to time, in a closed book environment, with no supplementary help (i.e. to simulate the real examination experience).

Practising your exam technique is also vitally important for you to assess your progress and identify areas of weakness that may need more attention in the final run up to the examination.

In order to achieve this we recognise that initially you may feel the need to practice some questions with open book help.

Good exam technique is vital.

...SION PLAN

...of strengths and weaknesses

THE KA...

Stage...

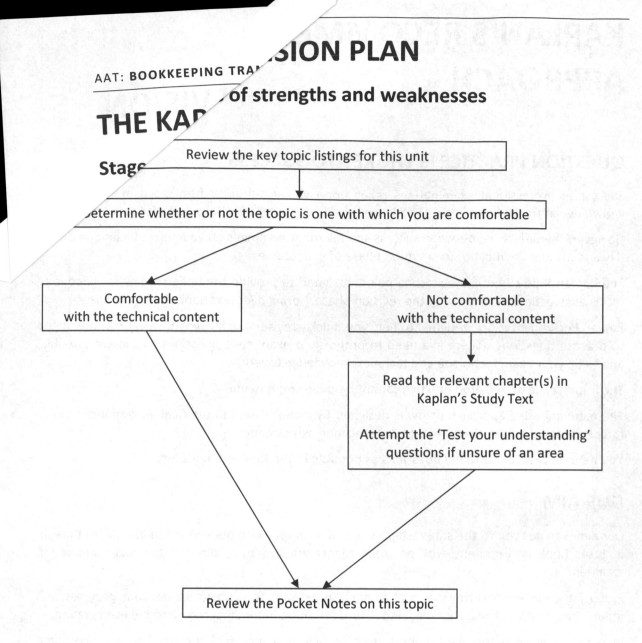

Review the key topic listings for this unit

↓

...etermine whether or not the topic is one with which you are comfortable

Comfortable
with the technical content

Not comfortable
with the technical content

Read the relevant chapter(s) in
Kaplan's Study Text

Attempt the 'Test your understanding'
questions if unsure of an area

Review the Pocket Notes on this topic

Stage 2: Practice questions

Follow the order of revision of topics as presented in this Kit and attempt the questions in the order suggested.

Try to avoid referring to Study Texts and your notes and the model answer until you have completed your attempt.

Review your attempt with the model answer and assess how much of the answer you achieved.

| Comfortable with question attempt | Not comfortable with question attempts |

Focus on these areas by:

- Reworking 'Test your understanding' questions in Kaplan's Study Text
- Revisiting the technical content from Kaplan's Pocket Notes
- Working any remaining questions on that area in the Exam Kit

Only revisit when comfortable with questions on all topic areas

Stage 3: Final pre-exam revision

We recommend that you **attempt at least one mock examination** containing a set of previously unseen exam-standard questions.

Attempt the mock CBA online in timed, closed book conditions to simulate the real exam experience.

Section 1

PRACTICE QUESTIONS

MAKING ENTRIES IN DAY BOOKS

1 SDB

Sales invoices have been prepared and partially entered in the sales day-book, as shown below.

(a) **Complete the entries in the sales day-book by inserting the appropriate figures for each invoice.**

(b) **Total the last five columns of the sales day-book.**

Sales day-book

Date 20XX	Details	Invoice number	Total £	VAT £	Net £	Sales type 1 £	Sales type 2 £
31 Dec	Poonams	105	3,600	600	3,000		3,000
31 Dec	D. Taylor	106	7,680	1,280	6,400	6,400	
31 Dec	Smiths	107	3,840	640	3,200		3,200
	Totals		15,120	2,520	12,600	6,400	6,200

2 FREDDIE LTD

Purchase invoices have been received and partially entered in the purchases day-book of Freddie Ltd, as shown below.

(a) **Complete the first two entries in the purchases day-book by inserting the appropriate figures for each invoice.**

(b) **Complete the final entry in the purchases day book by inserting the appropriate figures from the following invoice.**

Novot & Co

5 Pheasant Way, Essex, ES9 8BN

VAT Registration No. 453 098 541

Invoice No. 2176

Freddie Ltd

9 Banbury Street

Sheffield

31 July 20XX

10 boxes of product code 14212 @ £400 each	£4,000
VAT	£800
Total	£4,800
Payment terms 30 days	

Purchases day-book

Date 20XX	Details	Invoice number	Total £	VAT £	Net £	Product 14211 £	Product 14212 £
31 July	Box Ltd	2177	960	160	800	800	
31 July	Shrew Ltd	2175	14,400	2,400	12,000	12,000	
31 July	Novot & Co	2176	4,800	800	4,000		4,000
	Totals		20,160	3,360	16,800	12,800	4,000

3 MAHINDRA LTD

Sales invoices have been received and partially entered in the sales day-book of Mahindra Ltd, as shown below.

(a) Complete the entries in the sales day-book by inserting the appropriate figures for each invoice.

(b) Total the last five columns of the sales day-book.

Sales day-book

Date 20XX	Details	Invoice number	Total £	VAT £	Net £	Sales type 1 £	Sales type 2 £
31 Jan	Square Ltd	3567	1,200	200	1,000	1,000	
31 Jan	Oval & Co	3568	9,600	1,600	8,000		8,000
31 Jan	Diamond Ltd	3569	13,200	2,200	11,000		11,000
31 Jan	Triangle Ltd	3570	7,920	1,320	6,600	6,600	
	Totals		31,920	5,320	26,600	7,600	19,000

CODING

4 LEO LTD

Leo Ltd codes all sales invoices with a customer code AND a general ledger code. A selection of the codes used is given below.

Customer	Customer account code
DEF Ltd	DEF14
Gamma Production	GAM27
MBG Co	MBG20
Harley Interiors	HAR18
Clarkson Wholesale	CLA16

Item	General ledger code
Standard bath	GL529
Standard washbasin	GL526
Luxury taps	GL530
Bathroom cabinet	GL521
Toilet	GL535
Standard light switch	GL528

Leo Ltd
121 Apple Lane
Cuddington, CU9 8EF
VAT Registration No. 398 2774 01

DEF Ltd	
51 Neville Street,	18 Aug 20XX
Manchester, M1 4PJ	
10 .... Luxury taps for washbasin @ £8.80 each	£88.00
VAT	£17.60
Total	£105.60

(a)   **Select which codes would be used to code this invoice.**

General ledger code	Picklist: DEF14, GL529, GAM27, GL 526, GL530, GL521, GL535, CLA16
Customer account code	Picklist: GL530, GL526, DEF14, MBG20, HAR18, GL521, GL528, GAM27

(b)   **Why is it useful to use a customer code?**

Picklist: To help when inventory (stock) taking

To help when completing a tax return

To help find the total amount due to a supplier

To help trace orders and amounts due from particular customers

5   ELLA'S PAINTS

Ella's Paint's codes all purchases invoices with a supplier code AND a general ledger code. A selection of the codes used is given below.

Supplier	Supplier account code
Peak Ltd	PEA27
Marker Production	MAR19
MEG & Co	MEG20
Farley Interiors	FAR12
Hammond Wholesale	HAM16

Item	General ledger code
White Paint	GL360
Standard Roller	GL395
Standard Brush	GL320
Yellow Paint	GL370
Roller tray	GL330

This is an invoice received from a supplier.

Meg & Co
12 Barker Street
Leeds L1 4NZ
VAT Registration No. 402 2958 02

Ella's Paints	
19 Edmund St,	18 Feb 20XX
Newcastle, NE6 5DJ	
20 .... standard rollers @ £2.30 each	£46.00
VAT	£9.20
Total	£55.20

(a)   **Select which codes would be used to code this invoice.**

General ledger code	Picklist: PEA27, MAR19, GL360, MEG20, GL395, FAR12, GL330, HAM 16
Supplier account code	Picklist: PEA27, MAR19, GL360, MEG20, GL395, FAR12, GL330, HAM 16

(b)   **Why is it useful to use a supplier code?**

to help trace orders and amounts due from particular customers.

Picklist: To help when inventory (stock) taking

To help when completing a tax return

To help trace orders and amounts due to particular suppliers

To help trace orders and amounts due from particular customers

6 ROBERTO & CO

Roberto & Co codes all purchase invoices with a supplier code AND a general ledger code. A selection of the codes used is given below.

Supplier	Supplier account code
Alex Ltd	ALE1
Toyworld	TOY10
Pudding and Co	PUD4
Springclean Ltd	SPR7
Spoonaway	SPO3

Item	General ledger code
Food	GL18
Toys	GL72
Stationery	GL45
Cleaning Equipment	GL78
Kitchenware	GL29

This is an invoice received from a supplier.

Alex Ltd	
Cherry Way, Haworth, BD22 9HQ	
VAT Registration No. 248 2764 00	
Roberto & Co	
Roberto House	
Ashton, AS2 8TN	1 Jan 20XX
10 .... teddy bears @ £4 each	£40.00
VAT	£ 8.00
Total	£48.00

(a)   Select which codes would be used to code this invoice.

Supplier account code	Picklist: ALE1, TOY10, PUD4, SPR7, SPO3, GL18, GL72, GL45, GL78, GL29
General ledger code	Picklist: ALE1, TOY10, PUD4, SPR7, SPO3, GL18, GL72, GL45, GL78, GL29

(b) **Why is it necessary to use a general ledger code?**

To help calcubte expense incurred in a GL account

Picklist: To help when filling in a VAT return

To help when bar coding an item of inventory

To help find the total amount owing to a supplier ✓

To help calculate expense incurred in a GL account

TRANSFERRING DATA FROM DAY BOOKS TO LEDGERS

7 **LADY LTD**

Given below is the purchases day book for Lady Ltd

Date	Invoice No.	Code	Supplier	Total	VAT	Net
1 Dec	03582	PL210	M Brown	300.00	50.00	250.00
5 Dec	03617	PL219	H Madden	183.55	30.59	152.96
7 Dec	03622	PL227	L Singh	132.60	22.10	110.50
10 Dec	03623	PL228	A Stevens	90.00	15.00	75.00
18 Dec	03712	PL301	N Shema	197.08	32.84	164.24
			Totals	**903.23**	**150.53**	**752.70**

You are required to:

- Post the totals of the purchases day book to the general ledger accounts given

- Post the invoices to the payables' accounts in the subsidiary ledger given.

General ledger

Purchases ledger control account

	£		£
		1 Dec Balance b/d	5,103.90
		Purchases & VAT	903.23

VAT account

	£		£
PLCA	150.53	1 Dec Balance b/d	526.90

Purchases account

	£		£
1 Dec balance b/d	22,379.52		
PLCA	752.70		

Subsidiary ledger

M Brown

	£		£
		1 Dec Balance b/d	68.50
		PDB	302.00

H Madden

	£		£
		1 Dec Balance b/d	286.97
		PDB	133.55

L Singh

	£		£
		1 Dec Balance b/d	125.89
		PDB	132.60

A Stevens

	£		£
		1 Dec Balance b/d	12.36
		PDB	90.00

N Shema

	£		£
		1 Dec Balance b/d	168.70
		PDB	177.08

8 BUTTONS LTD

The following transactions all took place on 31 July and have been entered into the purchases day book of Buttons Ltd as shown below. No entries have yet been made into the ledger system.

Date 20XX	Details	Invoice number	Total £	VAT £	Net £
31 July	Peak & Co	1720	6,240	1,040	5,200
31 July	Max Ltd	1721	12,720	2,120	10,600
31 July	McIntyre Wholesale	1722	5,760	960	4,800
31 July	Pigmy Ltd	1723	3,744	624	3,120
	Totals		28,464	4,744	23,720

(a)   **What will be the entries in the purchases ledger?**

Account name	Amount £	Debit ✓	Credit ✓
Peak & Co	6,240		✓
Max Ltd	12,720		✓
McIntyre Wholesale	5,760		✓
Pigmy Ltd	3,744		✓

Picklist: Peak & Co, Purchases, Sales ledger control, Purchases returns, McIntyre Wholesale, Sales, Purchases ledger control, Max Ltd, Sales returns, VAT, Pigmy Ltd

(b)   **What will be the entries in the general ledger?**

Account name	Amount £	Debit ✓	Credit ✓
Purchases ledger account			✓
VAT		✓	
Purchases		✓	

Picklist: Purchases ledger control, Sales, Sales ledger control, Purchases, VAT

9   SPARKY LTD

The following credit transactions all took place on 31 July and have been entered into the sales returns day-book of Sparky Ltd as shown below. No entries have yet been made in the ledgers.

Sales returns day-book

Date 20XX	Details	Credit note number	Total £	VAT £	Net £
31 July	Clarkson Ltd	150C	1,680	280	1,400
31 July	Kyle & Co	151C	720	120	600
	Totals		2,400	400	2,000

(a)   **What will be the entries in the sales ledger?**

Sales ledger

Account name	Amount £	Debit ✓	Credit ✓
Clarkson Ltd	1,680		✓
Kyle & Co	720		✓

Picklist: Net, Purchases, Purchases ledger control, Clarkson Ltd, Purchases returns, Sales, Sales ledger control, Sales returns, Kyle & Co, Total, VAT

(b) **What will be the entries in the general ledger?**

General ledger

Account name	Amount £	Debit ✓	Credit ✓
Sales returns	2000	✓	✓
VAT	400	✓	
Sales ledger Control	2400		✓

Picklist: Kyle & Co, Net, Purchases, Purchases ledger control, Purchases returns, Sales, Sales ledger control, Sales returns, Clarkson Ltd, Total, VAT

10 LOUIS LTD

The following transactions all took place on 31 Jan and have been entered into the sales day book of Louis Ltd as shown below. No entries have yet been made into the ledger system.

Date 20XX	Details	Invoice number	Total £	VAT £	Net £
31 Jan	Sheep & Co	1400	3,840	640	3,200
31 Jan	Cow Ltd	1401	11,760	1,960	9,800
31 Jan	Chicken & Partners	1402	6,720	1,120	5,600
31 Jan	Pig Ltd	1403	14,496	2,416	12,080
	Totals		**36,816**	**6,136**	**30,680**

(a) **What will be the entries in the sales ledger?**

Account name	Amount £	Debit ✓	Credit ✓
Sheep & Co	3,840	✓	
Cow Ltd	11,760	✓	
Chicken & Partners	6,720	✓	
Pig Ltd	14,496	✓	

Picklist: Sheep & Co, Purchases, Sales ledger control, Cow Ltd, Purchases returns, Sales, Chicken & Partners, Purchases ledger control, Sales returns, VAT, Pig Ltd

(b) **What will be the entries in the general ledger?**

Account name	Amount £	Debit ✓	Credit ✓
Sales ledger control	36,816	✓	
VAT	6,136		✓
Sales	30,680		✓

Picklist: Purchases ledger control, Sales, Sales ledger control, Purchases, VAT

11 THOMAS & TILLY

The following credit transactions all took place on 31 Jan and have been entered into the purchase returns day-book of Thomas & Tilly as shown below. No entries have yet been made in the ledgers.

Purchase returns day-book

Date 20XX	Details	Credit note number	Total £	VAT £	Net £
31 Jan	May Ltd	230C	1,920	320	1,600
31 Jan	Hammond & Co	231C	1,200	200	1,000
	Totals		3,120	520	2,600

(a) **What will be the entries in the purchases ledger?**

Purchase ledger

Account name	Amount £	Debit ✓	Credit ✓
May Ltd	1,920	✓	
Hammond & Co	1,200	✓	

Picklist: Net, Purchases, Purchases ledger control, May Ltd, Purchases returns, Sales, Sales ledger control, Sales returns, VAT, Hammond & Co, Total.

(b) **What will be the entries in the general ledger?**

General ledger

Account name	Amount £	Debit ✓	Credit ✓
Purchases Ledger control	3,120	✓	
VAT	520		✓
Purchases returns	2,600		✓

Picklist: May Ltd, Net, Purchases, Purchases ledger control, Purchases returns, Sales, Sales ledger control, Sales returns, Hammond & Co, Total, VAT

12 FINCH'S

The following transactions all took place on 31 Dec and have been entered into the sales day book of Finch's as shown below. No entries have yet been made into the ledger system.

Date 20XX	Details	Invoice number	Total £	VAT £	Net £
31 Dec	Lou and Phil's	700	5,040	840	4,200
31 Dec	Eddie and Co	701	10,560	1,760	8,800
31 Dec	Noah's Arc	702	2,880	480	2,400
31 Dec	Alex and Freddie	703	720	120	600
	Totals		19,200	3,200	16,000

(a) **What will be the entries in the sales ledger?**

Account name	Amount £	Debit ✓	Credit ✓
Lou and Phil's	5,040	✓	
Eddie & Co	10,560	✓	
Noah's Arc	2,880	✓	
Alex and Freddie	720	✓	

Picklist: Lou and Phil's, Eddie and Co, Noah's Arc, Alex and Freddie, Purchases, Purchases ledger control, Purchases returns, Sales, Sales ledger control, Sales returns, VAT

(b) **What will be the entries in the general ledger?**

Account name	Amount £	Debit ✓	Credit ✓
Sales ledger control	16,200	✓	
VAT	3,200		✓
Sales	19,200		✓

Picklist: Purchases ledger control, Sales, Sales ledger control, Sales returns, VAT

13 JESSICA & CO

The following credit transactions all took place on 31 Dec and have been entered into the purchases returns day-book as shown below. No entries have yet been made in the ledgers.

Purchases returns day-book

Date 20XX	Details	Credit note number	Total £	VAT £	Net £
31 Dec	Iona Ltd	4763	1,680	280	1,400
31 Dec	Matilda Ltd	2164	4,320	720	3,600
	Totals		6,000	1,000	5,000

(a) **What will be the entries in the purchases ledger?**

Purchases ledger

Account name	Amount £	Debit ✓	Credit ✓
Iona Ltd	1,680	✓	
Matilda Ltd	4,320	✓	

Picklist: Iona Ltd, Matilda Ltd, Net, Purchases, Purchases ledger control, Purchases returns, Sales, Sales ledger control, Sales returns, Total, VAT

(b) **What will be the entries in the general ledger?**

General ledger

Account name	Amount £	Debit ✓	Credit ✓
Purchases ledger control	6,000	✓	
VAT	1,000		✓
Purchases returns	5,000		✓

Picklist: Iona Ltd, Matilda Ltd, Net, Purchases, Purchases ledger control, Purchases returns, Sales, Sales ledger control, Sales returns, VAT, Total

14 HORSEY REACH

The following transactions all took place on 31 July and have been entered into the discounts allowed day book of Horsey Reach as shown below. No entries have yet been made into the ledger system.

Date 20XX	Details	Credit note number	Total £	VAT £	Net £
31 July	Ashleigh Buildings	145	36.00	6.00	30.00
31 July	143 WGT	146	54.00	9.00	45.00
31 July	McDuff McGregor	147	43.20	7.20	36.00
31 July	Cameron Travel	148	93.60	15.60	78.00
	Totals		226.80	37.80	189.00

(a) **What will be the entries in the general ledger?**

Account name	Amount £	Debit ✓	Credit ✓
Sales ledger control	226.00	✓	✓
VAT	37.80	✓	✓
Discount allowed	189.00	✓	

Picklist: 13 WGT, Ashleigh Buildings, Cameron Travel, Discounts Allowed, Discounts Received, McDuff McGregor, Purchases, Purchases ledger control, Sales, Sales ledger control, VAT

(b) **What will be the entries in the subsidiary ledger?**

Account name	Amount £	Debit ✓	Credit ✓
Ashleigh Buildings	36.00		✓
143WGT	54.00		✓
McDuff McGregor	43.20		✓
Cameron travel	93.60		✓

Picklist: 143 WGT, Ashleigh Buildings, Cameron Travel, Discounts Allowed, Discounts Received, McDuff McGregor, Purchases, Purchases ledger control, Sales, Sales ledger control, VAT

15 BUTTERFLY BEES

These are the totals from the <u>discounts received</u> book of Butterfly Bees at the end of the month.

Total £	VAT £	Net £
427.20	71.20	356.00

(a) **What will be the entries in the general ledger?**

Account name	Amount £	Debit ✓	Credit ✓
Purchases ledger control	427.20	✓	
VAT	71.20		✓
Discounts received	356.00		✓

One of the entries in the discounts received day book is for a credit note received from Bella Bumps for £20 plus VAT.

(b) **What will be the entry in the purchases ledger?**

Account name	Amount £	Debit ✓	Credit ✓
Bella Bumps	24	✓	✓

16 OLIVIA ROSE BRIDAL SUPPLIES

These are the totals from the discounts allowed *sales* book of Olivia Rose Bridal Supplies at the end of the month.

Total £	VAT £	Net £
226.80	37.80	189.00

(a) **What will be the entries in the general ledger?**

Account name	Amount £	Debit ✓	Credit ✓
Sales ledger control	226.80		✓
VAT	37.80	✓	
Discount allowed	189.00	✓	

One of the entries in the discounts allowed day book is for a credit note sent to Bridezilla for £45 plus VAT.

(b) **What will be the entry in the sales ledger?**

Account name	Amount £	Debit ✓	Credit ✓
Bridezilla	54		✓

17 SUSSEX TRADING

These are the totals of the discounts allowed daybook of Sussex Trading at the end of the month.

Total £	VAT £	Net £
492.00	82.00	410.00

(a) What will be the entries in the general ledger?

Account name	Amount £	Debit ✓	Credit ✓
Discount allowed	410.00		✓
VAT	82.00		✓
Sales ledger control	492.00	✓	

One of the entries is for a credit note sent to Woody Woodburn for £65 plus VAT.

(b) What will be the entry in the sales ledger?

Account name	Amount £	Debit ✓	Credit ✓
Woody Woodburn	78	✓	

18 ROXY CAKE DESIGNS

These are the totals of the discounts allowed daybook of Roxy Cake Designs at the end of the month.

Total £	VAT £	Net £
381.60	63.60	318.00

(a) What will be the entries in the general ledger?

Account name	Amount £	Debit ✓	Credit ✓
Discount allowed	318.00	✓	
VAT	63.60	✓	
Sales ledger control	381.60		✓

One of the entries is for a credit note sent to Percy Tran for £28 plus VAT.

(b) What will be the entry in the sales ledger?

Account name	Amount £	Debit ✓	Credit ✓
Percy tran	33.6		✓

19 ANNANDALE SUPPLIES

These are the totals of the purchases returns daybook of Annandale Supplies at the end of the month.

Total £	VAT £	Net £
5,496.00	916.00	4,580.00

(a) Show the correct entries to be made in the general ledger by entering the correct account name and debit or credit next to each amount.

Account name	Amount £	Debit/Credit
Purchases returns	4,580.00	✓
VAT	916.00	✓
Purchases ledger control	5,496.00	✓

Picklist: Purchases / Sales / Sales returns / Purchases returns / Bank / VAT /Purchases ledger control / Sales ledger control / Debit / Credit

These are the totals of the sales returns daybook of Annandale Supplies at the end of the month.

Total £	VAT £	Net £
3,001.20	500.20	2,501.00

(b) Show the correct entries to be made in the general ledger by entering the correct account name and debit or credit next to each amount.

Account name	Amount £	Debit/Credit
Sales returns	2,501.00	✓
VAT	500.20	✓
Sales ledger Control	3,001.20	✓

Picklist: Purchases / Sales / Sales returns / Purchases returns / Bank / VAT /Purchases ledger control / Sales ledger control / Debit / Credit

20   NC CLEANING SUPPLIES

These are the totals from the purchases returns day book of NC Cleaning Supplies at the end of the month.

Total £	VAT £	Net £
318.00	53.00	265.00

(a)   **Show the entries to be made in the general ledger by selecting the correct account name and debit or credit option against each amount. You may use each option more than once.**

Account name	Amount £	Debit/Credit
Purchases ledger control	318.00	✓
VAT	53.00	✓
Purchases returns	265.00	✓

Options: Purchases, Purchases ledger control, Purchases returns, Sales, Sales ledger control, Sales returns, VAT, Debit, Credit

These are the totals from the sales returns day book of NC Cleaning Supplies at the end of the month.

Total £	VAT £	Net £
180.00	30.00	150.00

(b)   **Show the entries to be made in the general ledger by selecting the correct account name and debit or credit option against each amount. You may use each option more than once.**

Account name	Amount £	Debit/Credit
Sales ledger control	150.00	✓
VAT	30.00	✓
Sales returns	180.00	✓

Options: Purchases, Purchases ledger control, Purchases returns, Sales, Sales ledger control, Sales returns, VAT, Debit, Credit

THE CASH BOOK

21 ABC LTD

There are five payments to be entered in ABC Ltd's cash-book.

Receipts

| Received cash with thanks for goods bought.
From ABC Ltd, a customer without a credit account.

Net £180
VAT £36
Total £216

S. Lampard | Received cash with thanks for goods bought.
From ABC Ltd, a customer without a credit account.

Net £220
VAT £44
Total £264

S Bobbins | Received cash with thanks for goods bought.
ABC Ltd, a customer without a credit account.

Net £530
(No VAT)

Penny Rhodes |

Cheque book counterfoils

| Henley's Ltd
(Purchase ledger account HEN002)

£4,925

000372 | Epic Equipment Maintenance
(We have no credit account with this supplier)

£480 incl VAT

000373 |

(a) **Enter the details from the three receipts and two cheque book stubs into the credit side of the cash-book shown below and total each column.**

Cash-book – Credit side

Details	Cash	Bank	VAT	Payables	Cash purchases	Repairs and renewals
Balance b/f						
S. Lampard	216		36		180	
S. Bobbins	264		44		220	
Penny Rhodes	530				530	
Henley's Ltd		4,925		4,925		
Epic Equipment Maintenance		480	80			400
Total	1,010	5,405	160	4,925	930	400

There are two cheques from credit customers to be entered in ABC Ltd's cash book:

D. Davies £851

E. Denholm £450

(b) Enter the above details into the debit side of the cash-book and total each column.

Cash book – Debit side

Details	Cash	Bank	Receivables
Balance b/f	1,550	7,425	
D Davies		851	851
E Denholm		450	450
Total	1,550	8,726	1,301

(c) Using your answers to (a) and (b) above calculate the cash balance.

£ 540

(d) Using your answers to (a) and (b) above calculate the bank balance.

£ 8,321

(e) Will the bank balance calculated in (d) above be a debit or credit balance?

Debit/Credit

22 BEDS

There are five payments to be entered in Beds' cash-book.

Receipts

Received cash with thanks for goods bought. From Beds, a customer without a credit account. Net £590 VAT £118 Total £708 A. Blighty Ltd	Received cash with thanks for goods bought. From Beds, a customer without a credit account. Net £190 VAT £38 Total £228 R Bromby	Received cash with thanks for goods bought. From Beds, a customer without a credit account. Net £230 (No VAT) Roxy Bland

Cheque book counterfoils

Burgess Ltd (Purchase ledger account BUR003) £2,400 000101	Fast Equipment Repairs (We have no credit account with this supplier) £96 including VAT 000102

(a) Enter the details from the three receipts and two cheque book stubs into the credit side of the cash-book shown below and total each column.

Cash-book – Credit side

Details	Cash	Bank	VAT	Payables	Cash purchases	Repairs and renewals
Balance b/f						
A. Blighty Ltd	708		118		590	
R Bromby	228		38		190	
Roxy Bland	230				230	
Burgess Ltd		2,400		2,400		
Fast Equipment Repairs		96	16			80
Total	1,166	2,496	172	2,400	1,010	80

There are two cheques from credit customers to be entered in Beds' cash book:

A. Barnett   £698

H. Connelly   £250

(b) Enter the above details into the debit side of the cash-book and total each column.

Cash book – Sebit side

Details	Cash	Bank	Receivables
Balance b/f	1,175	3,825	
A Barnett		698	698
H Connelly		250	250
Total	1,175	4,773	948

(c) Using your answers to (a) and (b) above calculate the cash balance.

£   9

(d) Using your answers to (a) and (b) above calculate the bank balance.

£   2,277

(e) Will the bank balance calculated in (d) above be a debit or credit balance?

Debit/Credit

23   JO'S

There are five payments to be entered into Jo's cash-book.

Receipts

Received cash with thanks for good bought.	Received cash with thanks for good bought.	Received cash with thanks for good bought.
From Jo's, a customer without a credit account.	From Jo's, a customer without a credit account.	From Jo's, a customer without a credit account.
Net £40	Net £80	Net £455
VAT £8	VAT £16	(no VAT)
Total £48	Total £96	
T. Hunkin Ltd	Victoria Green	B. Head Ltd

Cheque book counterfoils

Smiths Ltd (Purchase ledger account SMI527) £4,250 001456	Arrow Valley Stationers (We have no credit account with this supplier) £120 (including VAT) 001457

(a)   **Enter the details from the three receipts and two cheque book stubs into the credit side of the cash-book shown below and total each column.**

Cash-book – credit side

Details	Cash	Bank	VAT	Payables	Cash purchases	Stationery expenses
Bal b/f		19,546				
T. Hunkin Ltd	48		8		40	
Victoria Green	96		16		80	
B. Head Ltd	455				455	
Smiths Ltd		4,250		4,250		
Arrow Valley Stationers		120	20			100
Total	599	23,916	44	4,250	575	100

There are two cheques from credit customers to be entered into Jo's cash book:

J Drummond   £623

N Atkinson   £425

(b)   Enter the above details into the debit side of the cash-book below and total each column.

Cash-book – debit side

Details	Cash	Bank	Receivables
Balance b/f	986		
J Drummond	623	623	623
N Atkinson		425	425
Total		1,048	1,048

(c)   Using your answers to (a) and (b) above calculate the cash balance.

£   387

(d)   Using your answers to (a) and (b) above calculate the bank balance.

£   22,868

(e)   Will the bank balance calculated in (d) above be a debit or a credit balance?

Debit/Credit

24   CHUGGER LTD

The following transactions all took place on 31 July and have been entered in the credit side of the cash-book as shown below. No entries have yet been made in the ledgers.

Cash-book – Credit side

Date 20XX	Details	VAT £	Bank £
31 July	Stationery	16	96
31 July	Photocopier repair	40	240

(a)   What will be the entries in the general ledger?

General ledger

Account name	Amount £	Debit ✓	Credit ✓
Stationery	96	✓	
Photocopier	240	✓	
VAT	56	✓	

Picklist: Stationery, Insurance, Repairs, Purchases ledger control, Sales ledger control, VAT

The following transactions all took place on 31 July and have been entered in the debit side of the cash-book as shown below. No entries have yet been made in the ledgers.

Cash-book – Debit side

Date 20XX	Details	Bank £
31 July	Balance b/f	6,350
31 July	BBG Ltd	7,200
31 July	EFG Ltd	5,000

(b) **What will be the TWO entries in the sales ledger?**

Sales ledger

Account name	Amount £	Debit ✓	Credit ✓
BBG Ltd	7,200		✓
EFG Ltd	5,000		✓

Picklist: Balance b/f, Sales ledger control, BBG Ltd, Purchases ledger control, EFG Ltd, Bank

(c) **What will be the entry in the general ledger?**

General ledger

Account name	Amount £	Debit ✓	Credit ✓
Sales ledger control	12,200		✓

Picklist: Balance b/f, EFG Ltd Purchase ledger control, Sales ledger control, VAT, Bank, BBG Ltd

25 ITALIAN STALLIONS

The following transactions all took place on 31 Jan and have been entered in the credit side of the cash-book of Italian Stallions Ltd as shown below. No entries have yet been made in the ledgers.

Cash-book – Credit side

Date 20XX	Details	VAT £	Bank £
31 Jan	Printer repair	32	192
31 Jan	Paper	16	96

(a)   **What will be the entries in the general ledger?**

General ledger

Account name	Amount £	Debit ✓	Credit ✓
Printer repair	192	✓	
Paper	96	✓	
VAT	48	✓	

Picklist: Repairs, Office supplies, Purchases ledger control, Sales ledger control, VAT

The following transactions all took place on 31 Jan and have been entered in the debit side of the cash-book as shown below. No entries have yet been made in the ledgers.

Cash-book – Debit side

Date 20XX	Details	Bank £
31 Jan	Balance b/f	5,100
31 Jan	AAG Ltd	4,000
31 Jan	HLG Ltd	3,000

(b)   **What will be the TWO entries in the sales ledger?**

Sales ledger

Account name	Amount £	Debit ✓	Credit ✓
AAG Ltd	4000		✓
HLG Ltd	3,000		✓

Picklist: Balance b/f, Sales ledger control, AAG Ltd, Purchases ledger control, HLG Ltd, Bank

(c)   **What will be the entry in the general ledger?**

General ledger

Account name	Amount £	Debit ✓	Credit ✓
Sales ledger control	7000		✓

Picklist: Balance b/f, EFG Ltd Purchase ledger control, Sales ledger control, VAT, Bank, BBG Ltd

26   FRED'S FISH

The following transactions all took place on 31 Dec and have been entered in the debit side of the cash-book as shown below. No entries have yet been made in the ledgers.

Cash-book – Debit side

Date 20XX	Details	Bank £
31 Dec	Balance b/f	4,280
31 Dec	K and D Ltd	8,200

(a)   What will be the entry in the sales ledger?

Sales ledger

Account name	Amount £	Debit ✓	Credit ✓
K and D Ltd	8,200		✓

Picklist: Balance b/f, Bank, Purchases ledger control, K and D Ltd, Sales ledger control

(b)   What will be the entry in the general ledger?

General ledger

Account name	Amount £	Debit ✓	Credit ✓
Sales ledger control	8,200		✓

Picklist: Balance b/f, Bank, Purchases ledger control, K and D Ltd, Sales ledger control

The following transactions all took place on 31 Dec and have been entered in the credit side of the cash-book as shown below. No entries have yet been made in the ledgers.

Cash-book – Credit side

Date 20XX	Details	VAT £	Bank £
31 Dec	Stationery	20	120
31 Dec	Postage		800

(c)   What will be the entries in the general ledger?

General ledger

Account name	Amount £	Debit ✓	Credit ✓
Stationery	120	✓	
Postage	800	✓	
VAT	20	✓	

Picklist: Bank, Postage, Stationery, Purchases ledger control, Sales ledger control, VAT

PETTY CASH

27   HICKORY HOUSE

Hickory House maintains a petty cash book as both a book of prime entry and part of the double entry accounting system. The following transactions all took place on 31 Dec and have been entered in the petty cash-book as shown below. No entries have yet been made in the general ledger.

Petty cash-book

Date 20XX	Details	Amount £	Date 20XX	Details	Amount £	VAT £	Postage £	Motor expenses £	Office expenses
31 Dec	Balance b/f	210.00	31 Dec	Stapler	6.72	1.12			5.60
31 Dec	Bank	90.00	31 Dec	Stamps	15.00		15.00		
			31 Dec	Parking	14.88	2.48		12.40	
			31 Dec	Stationery	19.20	3.20			16.00
			31 Dec	Balance c/d	244.20				
		300.00			300.00	6.80	15.00	12.40	21.60

What will be the FIVE entries in the general ledger?

General ledger

Account name	Amount £	Debit ✓	Credit ✓
VAT	6.80	✓	
Postage	15.00	✓	
Motor expenses	12.40	✓	
Office Expenses	21.60	✓	
Bank	300.00		✓

Picklist: Balance b/f, Balance c/d, Bank, Stationery, Stapler, Motor expenses, Parking, Office expenses, Petty cash-book, Stamps, Postage, VAT

28   MESSI & CO

Messi & Co maintains a petty cash book as a book of prime entry; it is not part of the double entry accounting system. The following transactions all took place on 31 Dec and have been entered in the petty cash-book as shown below. No entries have yet been made in the general ledger.

Petty cash-book

Date 20XX	Details	Amount £	Date 20XX	Details	Amount £	VAT £	Postage £	Motor expenses £	Office expenses
31 Dec	Op balance	100.00	31 Dec	Paper	27.33	4.55			22.78
			31 Dec	Stamps	4.50		4.50		
			31 Dec	Biscuits	6.60	1.10			5.50
			31 Dec	Parking	9.60	1.60		8.00	
			31 Dec	Cl balance	51.97				
		100.00			100.00	7.25	4.50	8.00	28.28

What will be the FIVE entries in the general ledger?

General ledger

Account name	Amount £	Debit ✓	Credit ✓
VAT	7.25	✓	
Postage	4.50	✓	
Motor expenses	8.50	✓	
Office Expenses	23.98	✓	
Petty cash control	100.00		✓

Picklist: Balance b/f, Balance c/d, Bank, Motor expenses, Paper, Parking, Petty cash control, Office expenses, Petty cash-book, Stamps, Postage, VAT

29 STAVROS

Stavros maintains a petty cash book as both a book of prime entry and part of the double entry accounting system. The following transactions all took place on 31 July and have been entered in the petty cash-book as shown below. No entries have yet been made in the general ledger.

Petty cash-book

Date 20XX	Details	Amount £	Date 20XX	Details	Amount £	VAT £	Sundry expenses £	Business travel £	Postage
1 July	Balance b/f	140	31 July	Newsagent	16.20	2.70	13.50		
31 July	Bank	110	31 July	Tea & Coffee	60.00	10.00	50.00		
			31 July	Business Travel	36.96	6.16		30.80	
			31 July	Postage	16.00				16.00
			31 July	Balance c/d	120.84				
		250.00			250.00	18.86	63.50	30.80	16.00

What will be the FIVE entries in the general ledger?

General ledger

Account name	Amount £	Debit ✓	Credit ✓
VAT	18.86	✓	
Sundry expenses	63.50	✓	
Business travel	30.80	✓	
Postage	16.00	✓	
Bank	250.00		✓

Picklist: Postage, Balance c/d, Bank, Fuel, Balance b/f, Motor repair, Sundry expenses, Petty cash-book, VAT, Business Travel

30 YUMMY CUPCAKES

Yummy Cupcakes maintains a petty cash book as a book of prime entry; it is not part of the double entry accounting system. The following transactions all took place on 31 July and have been entered in the petty cash-book as shown below. No entries have yet been made in the general ledger.

Petty cash-book

Date 20XX	Details	Amount £	Date 20XX	Details	Amount £	VAT £	Sundry expenses £	Business travel £	Postage
1 July	Op balance	150.00	31 July	Parking	15.00	2.50		12.50	
			31 July	Tea & Coffee	12.00	2.00	10.00		
			31 July	Travel	39.44	6.57		32.87	
			31 July	Stamps	4.00				4.00
			31 July	Cl balance	79.56				
		150.00			150.00	11.07	10.00	45.37	4.00

What will be the FIVE entries in the general ledger?

General ledger

Account name	Amount £	Debit ✓	Credit ✓
VAT	11.07	✓	
Sundry expenses	10.00	✓	
Business travel	45.37	✓	
Postage	4.00	✓	
Petty cash control	70.44		✓

Picklist: Postage, Balance c/d, Bank, Fuel, Balance b/f, Motor repair, Sundry expenses, Petty cash-book, VAT, Business Travel

31 OOH LA!

Ooh La! maintains a petty cash book as both a book of prime entry and part of the double entry accounting system. The following transactions all took place on 31 Jan and have been entered in the petty cash-book as shown below. No entries have yet been made in the general ledger.

Petty cash-book

Date 20XX	Details	Amount £	Date 20XX	Details	Amount £	VAT £	Sundry expenses £	Motor expense £	Postage
1 Jan	Balance b/f	80.00	31 Jan	Newsagent	12.30		12.30		
31 Jan	Bank	70.00	31 Jan	Post office	43.56	7.26			36.30
			31 Jan	Fuel	20.40	3.40		17.00	
			31 Jan	Tea & Coffee	27.30	4.55	22.75		
			31 Jan	Balance c/d	46.44				
		150.00			150.00	15.21	35.05	17.00	36.30

What will be the FIVE entries in the general ledger?

General ledger

Account name	Amount £	Debit ✓	Credit ✓
VAT	15.21	✓	
Sundry Expenses	35.05	✓	
Motor expenses	17.00	✓	
Postage	36.30	✓	
Bank	70.00		✓

Picklist: Postage, Balance c/d, Bank, Motor Expense, Balance b/f, Business Travel, Sundry expenses, Petty cash-book, VAT

32   QUEEN VIC

Part way through the month the petty cash account had a balance of £145.00. The cash in the petty cash box was checked and the following notes and coins were there.

Notes and coins	£
4 × £20 notes	80.00
1 × £10 notes	10.00
2 × £5 notes	10.00
12 × £1 coins	12.00
40 × 50p coins	20.00
45 × 20p coins	9.00

(a)   **Reconcile the cash amount in the petty cash box with the balance on the petty cash account.**

Amount in petty cash box	£ 141.00
Balance on petty cash account	£ 145.00
Difference	£ 4.00

At the end of the month the cash in the petty cash box was £27.25

(b)   **Complete the petty cash reimbursement document below to restore the imprest amount of £150.**

Petty cash reimbursement	
Date: 31.07.20XX	
Amount required to restore the cash in the petty cash box.	£ 122.75

33   THE ARCHES

This is a summary of petty cash payments made by The Arches.

Mick's Motors paid	£20.00 (no VAT)
Stamps paid	£19.00 (no VAT)
Office Essentials paid	£22.00 plus VAT

(a)   Enter the above transactions, in the order in which they are shown, in the petty cash-book below.

(b)   Total the petty cash-book and show the balance carried down.

Petty cash-book

Debit side		Credit side					
Details	Amount £	Details	Amount £	VAT £	Postage £	Travel £	Stationery £
Balance b/f	200.00	Mick's Motors	20.00			20.00	
		Stamps	19.00		19.00		
		Office Essentials	26.40	4.40			22.00
		Balance c/d	134.60				
	200.00		200.00	4.00	19.00	20.00	22.00

Picklist: Amount, Balance b/d, Balance c/d, Details, Postage, Stamps, Stationery, Office Essentials, Mick's Motors, VAT, Travel

34   RAINBOW

This is a summary of petty cash payments made by Rainbow.

Colin's Cabs paid	£28.00 (no VAT)
Post Office paid	£18.00 (no VAT)
ABC Stationery paid	£32.00 plus VAT

(a)   Enter the above transactions, in the order in which they are shown, in the petty cash-book below.

(b)   Total the petty cash-book and show the balance carried down.

Petty cash-book

Debit side		Credit side					
Details	Amount £	Details	Amount £	VAT £	Postage £	Travel £	Stationery £
Balance b/f	100.00	Colin's Cabs	28.00			28.00	
		Post Office	18.00		18.00		
		ABC Stationery	38.40	6.40			32.00
		Balance c/d	15.60				
	100.00		100.00	6.40	18.00	28.00	32.00

Picklist: Amount, Balance b/d, Balance c/d, Details, Postage, Post Office, Stationery, ABC Stationery, Colin's Cabs, VAT, Travel

35 SOOTY & SWEEP

Part way through the month the petty cash account had a balance of £135.00. The cash in the petty cash box was checked and the following notes and coins were there.

Notes and coins	£
2 × £20 notes	40.00
6 × £10 notes	60.00
15 × £1 coins	15.00
18 × 50p coins	9.00
12 × 20p coins	2.40
10 × 10p coins	1.00

(a) **Reconcile the cash amount in the petty cash box with the balance on the petty cash account.**

Amount in petty cash box	£ 127·40
Balance on petty cash account	£ 135.00
Difference	£ 7·60

At the end of the month the cash in the petty cash box was £5.00

(b) **Complete the petty cash reimbursement document below to restore the imprest amount of £250.**

Petty cash reimbursement	
Date: 31.07.20XX	
Amount required to restore the cash in the petty cash box.	£ 245.00

36 JAWS DENTISTRY

This is a summary of petty cash payments made by Jaws Dentistry.

Ace Taxis paid	£26.00 (no VAT)
Kate's Couriers	£27.00 (no VAT)
Smiths Stationery	£38.00 plus VAT

(a) **Enter the above transactions, in the order in which they are shown, in the petty cash-book below.**

(b) **Total the petty cash-book and show the balance carried down.**

Petty cash-book

Debit side		Credit side					
Details	Amount £	Details	Amount £	VAT £	Postage £	Travel £	Stationery £
Balance b/f	225.00	Ace taxis	26.00			26.00	
		Kate's Couriers	27.00		27.00		
		Smiths Stationery	45.60	7.60			38.00
		Balance c/d	126.40				
	225.00		225.00	7.60	27.00	26.00	38.00

Picklist: Amount, Balance b/d, Balance c/d, Details, Postage, Kate's Couriers, Smiths Stationery, Ace Taxis, Travel, VAT.

37 TOM'S TILES

Part way through the month the petty cash account had a balance of £165.52. The cash in the petty cash box was checked and the following notes and coins were there.

Notes and coins	£
4 × £20 notes	80.00
4 × £10 notes	40.00
3 × £5 notes	15.00
18 × £1 coins	18.00
7 × 50p coins	3.50
18 × 20p coins	3.60
19 × 10p coins	1.90
6 × 2p coins	0.12

(a) **Reconcile the cash amount in the petty cash box with the balance on the petty cash account.**

Amount in petty cash box	£ 162.12
Balance on petty cash account	£ 165.52
Difference	£ 3.40

At the end of the month the cash in the petty cash box was £25.88.

(b) Complete the petty cash reimbursement document below to restore the imprest amount of £250.00.

Petty cash reimbursement	
Date: 30.04.20XX	
Amount required to restore the cash in the petty cash box.	£ 224·12

38 ROCKY RILEY

This is a summary of petty cash payments made by Rocky Riley.

Kath's Kars paid	£32.00 (no VAT)
Stamps paid	£25.00 (no VAT)
Pauline's Pens paid	£20.00 plus VAT

(a) Enter the above transactions, in the order in which they are shown, in the petty cash-book below.

(b) Total the petty cash-book and show the balance carried down.

Petty cash-book

Debit side		Credit side					
Details	Amount £	Details	Amount £	VAT £	Postage £	Travel £	Stationery £
Balance b/f	175.00	Kath's Kars	32.00			32.00	
		Stamps	25.00		25.00		
		Pauline's Pen	24.00	4.00			20.00
		Balance c/d	94.00				
	175.00		175.00	4.00	25.00	32.00	20.00

Picklist: Amount, Balance b/d, Balance c/d, Details, Postage, Stamps, Stationery, Pauline's Pens, Kath's Kars, Travel, VAT

39 MHAIRI MOTORS

Part way through the month the petty cash account had a balance of £110.00. The cash in the petty cash box was checked and the following notes and coins were there.

Notes and coins	£
5 × £10 notes	50.00
5 × £5 notes	25.00
4 × £1 coins	4.00
11 × 50p coins	5.50
75 × 20p coins	15.00
3 × 10p coins	0.30

99.80

(a) **Reconcile the cash amount in the petty cash box with the balance on the petty cash account.**

Amount in petty cash box	£ 99.80
Balance on petty cash account	£ 110.00
Difference	£ 10.2

At the end of the month the cash in the petty cash box was £8.50

(b) **Complete the petty cash reimbursement document below to restore the imprest amount of £200.**

Petty cash reimbursement	
Date: 31.07.20XX	
Amount required to restore the cash in the petty cash box.	£ 191.50

40 DAINTY DESIGNS

Dainty Designs keeps an analytical petty cash book.

On 31 March there was one final petty cash payment to be recorded in the petty cash book.

An amount of £31.20 including VAT had been paid for fuel expenses.

(a) **Calculate the VAT and net amounts to be recorded in the petty cash book.**

VAT £	Net £
5.20	26.00

Before the petty cash payment in (a) was recorded, amounts totalling £65.66 had been entered into the fuel expenses analysis column of the petty cash book.

nett 26 =91.66

(b) **Calculate the total of the fuel expenses analysis column after the petty cash payment in (a) has been recorded.**

£ 91.66

After all March petty cash payments had been made, an amount of £42.30 was left in the petty cash float.

This agreed with the total of all payments now recorded in the petty cash book of £233.90. On 31 March the petty cash float was topped up to £280.

(c) **What will be the entry in the petty cash book to record this transaction?**

Details	Amount £	Debit ✓	Credit ✓
Cash from bank	237.70	✓	

Picklist: Balance b/d, Balance c/d, Cash from bank

(d) **What will be the entry in the petty cash book to record the closing balance on 31 March?**

Details	Amount £	Debit ✓	Credit ✓
Balance c/d	280.00		✓

Picklist: Balance b/d, Balance c/d, Cash from bank

On 2 April the following petty cash vouchers are ready to be recorded:

Petty cash voucher 222

2 April 20X7

Diesel

£27.00 plus VAT

Petty cash voucher 223

2 April 20X7

Lever arch files

£12.00 including VAT

(e) **What will be the total, VAT and net amounts to be entered into the petty cash book?**

Petty cash voucher	Total £	VAT £	Net £
222	32.40	5.40	27.00
223	14.40	2.40	12.00

41 JACKSON MOTORING

Jackson Motoring keeps an analytical petty cash book.

On 31 October there was one final petty cash payment to be recorded in the petty cash book.

An amount of £21.60 including VAT had been paid for stationery expenses.

(a) **Calculate the VAT and net amounts to be recorded in the petty cash book.**

VAT £	Net £
3.60	18

Before the petty cash payment in (a) was recorded, amounts totalling £15.50 had been entered into the stationery expenses analysis column of the petty cash book.

(b) **Calculate the total of the stationery expenses analysis column after the petty cash payment in (a) has been recorded.**

£ 33.50

After all October petty cash payments had been made, an amount of £31.55 was left in the petty cash float.

This agreed with the total of all payments now recorded in the petty cash book of £152.40. On 31 October the petty cash float was topped up to £215.

(c)   **What will be the entry in the petty cash book to record this transaction?**

Details	Amount £	Debit ✓	Credit ✓
Cash from Bank	183.45	✓	

Picklist: Balance b/d, Balance c/d, Cash from bank

(d)   **What will be the entry in the petty cash book to record the closing balance on 31 October?**

Details	Amount £	Debit ✓	Credit ✓
Balance c/d	215		✓

Picklist: Balance b/d, Balance c/d, Cash from bank

On 2 November the following petty cash vouchers are ready to be recorded:

Petty cash voucher 120

2 November 20X7

FST Taxis

£20 (no VAT)

Petty cash voucher 121

2 November 20X7

Pens

£19.20 including VAT

(e)   **What will be the total, VAT and net amounts to be entered into the petty cash book?**

Petty cash voucher	Total £	VAT £	Net £
120	20	0	20
121	19.20	3.20	16.00

42 LJ INTERIORS

These are the totals of the petty cash book at the end of the month.

Details	Amount £	Details	Amount £	VAT £	Stationery £	Postage £	Charitable donations £
Total	566	Totals	566	64	320	32	150

What will be the entries in the general ledger?

Account name	Amount £	Debit ✓	Credit ✓
VAt	64	✓	
Stationery	320	✓	
Postage	32	✓	
Charitable donations	150	✓	

43 KAZ KARATE CLUB

These are the totals of the petty cash book at the end of the month.

Details	Amount £	Details	Amount £	VAT £	Motor expenses £	Postage £	Insurance £
Total	386	Totals	386	31	155	20	180

What will be the entries in the general ledger?

Account name	Amount £	Debit ✓	Credit ✓
VAT	31	✓	
Motor expenses	155	✓	
Postage	20	✓	
Insurance	180	✓	

44   JACINTA INTERIOR DESIGN

The petty cash at Jacinta Interior Design is restored to £300 at the end of each week. The following amounts were paid out of petty cash during week 22:

Stationery	£42.30 including VAT at 20%
Travelling costs	£76.50
Office refreshments	£38.70
Sundry payables	£72.00 plus VAT at 20%

(a)   **Complete the petty cash reimbursement document below to restore the imprest amount of £300.**

Petty cash reimbursement	
Week 22 Amount required to restore the cash in the petty cash box.	£ 243.90

(b)   **Which one of the following states the entries required to account for the reimbursement to the petty cash float from the bank account?**

A	Dr Petty cash	Cr Bank
B	Dr Bank	Cr Petty cash
C	Dr Drawings	Cr Petty cash
D	Dr Drawings	Cr Bank

45   MARTHA

Martha maintains a petty cash book as both a book of prime entry and part of the double entry accounting system. The petty cash book below has been partly completed for the month of April.

Petty cash-book

Date 20XX	Details	Amount £	Date 20XX	Details	Amount £	VAT £	Cleaning expenses £	Motor expenses £	Office expenses £
01 Apr	Bank	150.00	11 Apr	Cleaning supplies	14.88	2.48	12.40		
			12 Apr	Stationery	42.48	7.08			35.40
					57.36	9.56	12.40		35.40

On 30th April there was one final petty cash payment for the month to be recorded:

Cleaning Services Ltd   £60 including VAT.

(a)   **Calculate the VAT and net amounts of this petty cash payment to be recorded in the petty cash book.**

VAT £	Net £
10	50

(b)   Calculate the total of the cleaning expense analysis column after taking into consideration the petty cash payment in (a).

£   62.40

(c)   After taking into consideration the transaction in (a) what will be the entry in the petty cash book to restore to the imprest level of £150.

Details	Amount £	Debit ✓	Credit ✓
Cash from Bank	117.36	✓	

Details picklist: Amount, Balance b/d, Balance c/d, Cash from bank

(d)   What is the entry made in the petty cash book to record the closing balance on 30th April?

Details	Amount £	Debit ✓	Credit ✓
Balance c/d	150.00		✓

Details picklist: Amount, Balance b/d, Balance c/d, Cash from bank

The following petty cash receipts need to be recorded in the petty cash book for the month of May.

98	99	100
Newark Printers	**ERJ Motor Supplies**	**Co-pop**
Printer ink	Wiper blades	Cleaning products
£17.40 including VAT at 20%.	£38.40 inclusive of VAT at 20%.	£6.00 gross of £1.00 VAT.

(e)   For each receipt identify the analysis column to be used for the payment and the amount of the transaction that should be recorded in the analysis column.

Petty cash receipt	Analysis column	Amount £
Newark Printers	Office expenses	14.50
ERJ Motor Supplies	Motor expenses	32.00
Co-pop	Cleaning expenses	6.00

Analysis column picklist: Cleaning expenses, Motor expenses, Office expenses

DRAFTING AN INITIAL TRIAL BALANCE

46   BROOKLYN BOATS

The following two accounts are in the general ledger of Brooklyn Boats at the close of day on 31 Dec.

(a)   **Insert the balance carried down together with date and details.**

(b)   **Insert the totals.**

(c)   **Insert the balance brought down together with date and details.**

Electricity

Date 20XX	Details	Amount £	Date 20XX	Details	Amount £
01 Dec	Balance b/f	870	31 Dec	Balance c/d	1,220
12 Dec	Bank	350			
	Total	1220		Total	1,220
1 Jan	Balance b/d	1220			

Picklist: Balance b/d, Balance c/d, Bank, Closing balance, Opening balance, Purchases ledger control

Discounts received

Date 20XX	Details	Amount £	Date 20XX	Details	Amount £
31 Dec	Balance c/d	600	1 Dec	Bal b/f	500
			15 Dec	Purchase ledger control	100
	Total	600		Total	600
			1 Jan	Balance b/d	600

Picklist: Balance b/d, Balance c/d, Bank, Closing balance, Opening balance, Sales ledger control

47   WIGGLE POGGLE LTD

The following two accounts are in the general ledger of Wiggle Poggle Ltd at the close of day on 31 July.

(a)   Insert the balance carried down together with date and details.

(b)   Insert the totals.

(c)   Insert the balance brought down together with date and details.

Discount allowed

Date 20XX	Details	Amount £	Date 20XX	Details	Amount £
01 July	Balance b/f	1,560	31 Aug.	Balance c/d	2,160
14 July	Sales ledger control account (SLCA)	480			
16 July	Sales ledger control account (SLCA)	120			
	Total	2160		Total	2,160
1 Aug	Balance b/d	2160			

Picklist: Balance b/d, Balance c/d, Bank, Closing balance, Opening balance, Sales ledger control

Interest income

Date 20XX	Details	Amount £	Date 20XX	Details	Amount £
31 July	Balance c/d	400	01 July	Balance b/f	320
			28 July	Bank	80
	Total	400		Total	
			1 Aug	Balance b/d	400

Picklist: Balance b/d, Balance c/d, Bank, Closing balance, Opening balance, Sales ledger control

48   CRAZY CURTAINS

The following two accounts are in the general ledger of Crazy Curtains at the close of day on 31 Jan.

(a)   **Insert the balance carried down together with date and details.**

(b)   **Insert the totals.**

(c)   **Insert the balance brought down together with date and details.**

Electricity expense

Date 20XX	Details	Amount £	Date 20XX	Details	Amount £
01 Jan	Bal b/f	200	31 Jan	Balance c/d	450
22 Jan	Bank	250			
	Total	450		Total	450
1 Feb	balance b/d	450			

Picklist: Balance b/d, Balance c/d, Bank, Closing balance, Opening balance, Electricity Expense

Rental income

Date 20XX	Details	Amount £	Date 20XX	Details	Amount £
31 Jan	Balance c/d	1000	01 Jan	Balance b/f	400
			28 Jan	Bank	600
	Total	1000		Total	
			1 Feb	Balance b/d	1000

Picklist: Balance b/d, Balance c/d, Bank, Closing balance, Opening balance, Sales ledger control

49 SMITH & SON

Below is a list of balances to be transferred to the trial balance of Smith & Son at 31 Dec.

Place the figures in the debit or credit column, as appropriate, and total each column.

Account name	Amount £	Debit £	Credit £
Fixtures and fittings	8,250	8,250	
Capital	18,400		18,400
Bank overdraft	4,870		4,870
Petty cash control	350	350	
Sales ledger control (SLCA)	42,870	42,870	
Purchases ledger control (PLCA)	23,865		23,865
VAT owed to tax authorities	10,245		10,245
Inventory	9,870	9,870	
Loan from bank	22,484		22,484
Sales	180,264		180,264
Sales returns	5,420	5,420	
Purchases	129,030	129,030	
Purchases returns	2,678		2,678
Discount allowed D	2,222	2,222	
Discount received C	3,432		3,432
Heat and Light	1,490	1,490	
Motor expenses	2,354	2,354	
Wages	42,709	42,709	
Rent and rates	10,600	10,600	
Repairs	3,020	3,020	
Hotel expenses	1,890	1,890	
Telephone	2,220	2,220	
Delivery costs	1,276	1,276	
Miscellaneous expenses	2,667	2,667	
Totals		266,238	266,238

50 EXPIALIDOCIOUS LTD

Below is a list of balances to be transferred to the trial balance of Expialidocious Ltd as at 31 July.

Place the figures in the debit or credit column, as appropriate, and total each column.

Account name	Amount £	Debit £	Credit £
Capital	25,360		25,360
Petty cash control	250	250	
Loan from bank	11,600		11,600
Sales ledger control (SLCA)	159,242	159,242	
Purchases ledger control (PLCA)	83,682		83,682
Motor vehicles	35,900	35,900	
Inventory	28,460	28,460	
Bank overdraft	10,063		10,063
VAT owed from tax authorities	15,980	15,980	
Purchases	343,014	343,014	
Purchases returns	1,515		1,515
Wages	56,150	56,150	
Motor expenses	2,950	2,950	
Interest income	400		400
Sales	532,900		532,900
Sales returns	5,760	5,760	
Stationery	1,900	1,900	
Light & heat	6,500	6,500	
Discount received	200		200
Discount allowed	2,160	2,160	
Interest paid on overdraft	550	550	
Travel	1,800	1,800	
Marketing	650	650	
Telephone	1,510	1,510	
Miscellaneous expenses	2,944	2,944	
Totals		665,720	665,720

51   DIXON FURNITURE

Below is a list of balances to be transferred to the trial balance of Dixon Furniture as at 31 Jan.

Place the figures in the debit or credit column, as appropriate, and total each column.

Account name	Amount £	Debit £	Credit £
Motor vehicles	40,100	40,100	
Capital	35,000		35,000
Petty cash control	150	150	
Bank balance	14,654	14,654	
Wages	37,890	37,890	
Travel expenses	1,500	1,500	
Rental income	1,000	1,000	1,000
Sales	435,600		435,600
Loan from bank	10,000		10,000
Sales ledger control (SLCA)	127,456	127,456	
Inventory	22,500	22,500	
Purchases ledger control (PLCA)	91,250		91,250
VAT due to tax authorities	12,500		12,500
Purchases	325,600	325,600	
Sales returns	6,500	6,500	
Purchases returns	1,250		1,250
Sundry expenses	3,600	3,600	
Electricity expense	450	450	
Bank interest received	360		360
Fuel expense	900	900	
Discount received	600		600
Discount allowed	1,560	1,560	
Advertising	300	300	
Telephone	1,900	1,900	
Miscellaneous expenses	2,500	2,500	
Totals		587,560	587,560

52 BALANCES (1)

The following four accounts are in the general ledger at close of day on 31 December.

Capital

Date 20XX	Details	Amount £	Date 20XX	Details	Amount £
			01 Dec	Balance b/f	5,000
			25 Dec	Bank	1,000

Fixtures and Fittings

Date 20XX	Details	Amount £	Date 20XX	Details	Amount £
01 Dec	Balance b/f	18,500	8 Dec	Journal	1,200
12 Dec	Bank	2,500			

Loan

Date 20XX	Details	Amount £	Date 20XX	Details	Amount £
31 Dec	Bank	1,650	1,650	Balance b/f	24,880

Drawings

Date 20XX	Details	Amount £	Date 20XX	Details	Amount £
01 Dec	Balance b/f	1,800			
20 Dec	Bank	650			

Record the totals and balances of each account in the table below by:

- inserting the balance carried down at 31 December,

- showing whether the balance carried down will be a debit or a credit, and

- inserting the total that will be shown in both the debit and credit columns after the account has been balanced.

Account name	Balance c/d at 31 December £	Debit/Credit	Total shown in both the debit and credit columns £
Capital	6000	✓	6000
Fixtures and Fittings	19800	✓	21,000
Loan	23,230	✓	24,880
Drawings	2490	✓	2,490

53 BALANCES (2)

The following four accounts are in the general ledger at close of day on 31 March.

Capital

Date 20XX	Details	Amount £	Date 20XX	Details	Amount £
			01 Mar	Balance b/f	10,000
			25 Mar	Bank	5,000

Plant and Machinery

Date 20XX	Details	Amount £	Date 20XX	Details	Amount £
01 Mar	Balance b/f	8,500	8 Mar	Journal	800
12 Mar	Bank	1,250			

Loan

Date 20XX	Details	Amount £	Date 20XX	Details	Amount £
31 Mar	Bank	1,020	01 Mar	Balance b/f	15,200

Drawings

Date 20XX	Details	Amount £	Date 20XX	Details	Amount £
01 Mar	Balance b/f	3,330			
20 Mar	Bank	890			

Record the totals and balances of each account in the table below by:

- inserting the balance carried down at 31 March,

- showing whether the balance carried down will be a debit or a credit, and

- inserting the total that will be shown in both the debit and credit columns after the account has been balanced.

Account name	Balance c/d at 31 March £	Debit/Credit	Total shown in both the debit and credit columns £
Capital	15000	✓	15000
Plant and Machinery	8950	✓	9750
Loan	14,180	✓	15,200
Drawings	4220	✓	4,220.

54 ARCHIE

Below are the balances of the debit and credit columns of Archie's partially prepared trial balance. As the trial balance is not yet complete it does not balance.

Debit £	Credit £
31,150	
	87,000
4,050	
58,920	
	1,700
11,075	
	23,111
6,250	
3,990	111 811

115,435

(a) **Calculate the total of each of the debit and credit columns of the partially complete trial balance.**

Debit £	Credit £
115,435	111,811

118,670

There are now three final balances to be transferred to the trial balance.

Account name	Balance £
Drawings D	2,350
Purchases ledger control C	6,859
Discounts allowed D	885

(b) **Transfer each balance to the debit or credit column of the trial balance extract below.**

Account name	Debit £	Credit £
Drawings	2,350	
Purchases ledger control		6,859
Discounts allowed	885	

The trial balance should now balance.

(c) **Calculate the final total to be entered into the debit and credit columns of the trial balance.**

£ 118,670

The trial balance for a different organisation is being prepared.

These are the balances available so far:

Sales ledger accounts	Balance £
Original Ltd	8,900
Evie & Joe	10,880

Purchases ledger accounts	Balance £
Jacob & Danny	1,280
PPR LLP	6,122

General ledger accounts	Balance £
Fixtures and Fittings	29,000
Capital	60,500
Discounts allowed	1,035
Rent received	13,670
Bank (in funds)	12,600
Sales	145,000

(d)   Identify SIX accounts that will appear in the trial balance and whether they will be transferred to the debit or credit column.

Account name	Debit ✓	Credit ✓	Does not appear in the trial balance ✓
Fixtures and fittings	29,000		
Capital		60,500	
Discounts allowed	1,035		
Rent received		13,670	
Bank	12,600		
Sales		145000	
Original Ltd			✓
Evie & Joe			✓
Jacob & Danny			✓
PPR LLP			✓

55   HARRISON

Below are the balances of the debit and credit columns of Harrison's partially prepared trial balance. As the trial balance is not yet complete it does not balance.

Debit £	Credit £
28,230	
	95,000
670	
61,000	
	835
9,423	
	17,555
5,800	
4,032	

(a)   **Calculate the total of each of the debit and credit columns of the partially complete trial balance.**

Debit £	Credit £
109,155	113,370

There are now three final balances to be transferred to the trial balance.

Account name	Balance £
Drawings	8,000
Capital	3,315
Discounts received	450

(b)   **Transfer each balance to the debit or credit column of the trial balance extract below.**

Account name	Debit £	Credit £
Drawings	8000	
Capital		3,315
Discounts received		450

The trial balance should now balance.

(c)   **Calculate the final total to be entered into the debit and credit columns of the trial balance.**

£   117,155

The trial balance for a different organisation is being prepared.

These are the balances available so far:

Sales ledger accounts	Balance £
Dave & Malc Co	3,120
Amy & Molly	4,500

Purchases ledger accounts	Balance £
Peter & Paul	8,000
Morris Ltd	4,500

General ledger accounts	Balance £
Motor vehicles	22,550
Capital	45,000
Discounts received	450
Interest paid	660
Bank overdraft	6,700
Purchases	6,000

(d) **Identify SIX accounts that will appear in the trial balance and whether they will be transferred to the debit or credit column**

Account name	Debit ✓	Credit ✓	Does not appear in the trial balance ✓
Motor vehicles	✓		
Capital		✓	
Discounts received		✓	
Interest paid	✓		
Bank overdraft		✓	
Purchases	✓		
Dave & Malc Co			✓
Amy & Molly			✓
Peter & Paul			✓
Morris Ltd			✓

56 KOOKABURRA

Below is an extract of balances from Kookaburra's trial balance.

(a) **Calculate and insert the total of each of the debit and credit columns of the partially prepared trial balance.**

Account name	Debit £	Credit £
Plant and equipment	106,340	
Sales ledger control (SLCA)	36,470	
Bank	12,590	
Inventory	18,240	
Purchases ledger control (PLCA)		27,021
Capital		50,000
Bank loan		2,590
Sales		625,640
Purchases	295,100	
Wages	32,410	
Administrative expenses	1,280	
Rent and rates	12,490	
Heat and light	4,291	
Entertainment expenses	456	
Telephone and broadband expenses	3,214	
Totals	522,881	705,251

Shown below are the three final balances to be transferred to the trial balance.

(b) **Transfer each balance to the debit or credit column of the trial balance extract below.**

Account name	Amount £	Debit £	Credit £
Purchases returns	14,980		14,980
Land and Buildings	197,000	197,000	
Petty cash	350	350	

The trial balance should now balance meaning the totals of the debit and credit columns should agree.

(c) **Calculate the final total entered into the debit and credit columns of the trial balance.**

£   720,231

The trial balance for a different organisation is being prepared and balances have been provided from the accounting records.

(d) **You are required to identify whether these accounts appear in the trial balance and if so whether they would be transferred to the debit or credit column.**

Sales ledger

Account name	Account balance	Transfers to the trial balance in the DEBIT column ✓	Transfers to the trial balance in the CREDIT column ✓	Does not transfer to the trial balance ✓
Riley Racing	£3,250			✓
Kat's Cakes	£2,560			✓

Purchases ledger

Account name	Account balance	Transfers to the trial balance in the DEBIT column ✓	Transfers to the trial balance in the CREDIT column ✓	Does not transfer to the trial balance ✓
VK Supplies	£2,364			✓
TAF Ltd	£7,171			✓

General ledger

Account name	Account balance	Transfers to the trial balance in the DEBIT column ✓	Transfers to the trial balance in the CREDIT column ✓	Does not transfer to the trial balance ✓
Sales returns	£23,910	✓		
Bank overdraft	£2,185		✓	

57   **ALAN**

The following are the year end balances in Alan's general ledger:

	£
Sales	628,000
Cost of sales	458,000
General expenses	138,000
Purchases ledger control	54,000
Sales ledger control	?
Bank (in funds)	61,000
Capital	86,000

(a)   **If Alan's trial balance balances, what is the missing figure for the sales ledger control?**

A   £61,000

B   £111,000

C   £233,000

D   £387,000

(b)   **Taking into consideration the answer to part (a) what is the trial balance total?**

£   768,000

(c)   **Which of the following balances would appear on the same side in the trial balance?**

A   Drawings and bank loan

B   Drawings and purchases

C   Capital and purchases

D   Capital and rental expense

DOCUMENTATION AND RECORDS FOR SUPPLIERS

58   NAN NURSING

A supply of chocolate puddings have been delivered to Nan Nursing by Pudding and Co. The purchase order sent from Nan Nursing, and the invoice from Pudding and Co, are shown below.

Nan Nursing

22 Nursery Road

Keighley, BD22 7BD

Purchase Order No. HH72

To: Pudding and Co

Date: 15 August 20XX

Please supply 50 chocolate puddings product code 742087

Purchase price: £20 per 10, plus VAT

Discount: less 10% trade discount, as agreed.

Pudding and Co

17 Pudding Lane, Bradford, BD19 7HX

VAT Registration No. 234 7654 00

Invoice No. 428

Nan Nursing

22 Nursery Road

Keighley, BD22 7BD

20 August 20XX

50 .... chocolate puddings product code 742087 @ £2 each	£50
Less Trade Discount	£10
Net	£40
VAT	£ 8
Total	£48
Terms: 30 days net	

Check the invoice against the purchase order and answer the following questions.

Has the correct purchase price of the chocolate puddings been charged?   Y / <u>N</u>

Has the correct total discount been calculated?   <u>Y</u> / N

What would be the VAT amount charged if the invoice was correct?   £ ___18___

What would be the total amount charged if the invoice was correct?   £ __108__

59 **PIXIE PAPERS**

A supply of paper has been delivered to Alpha Ltd by Pixie Paper. The purchase order sent from Alpha Ltd, and the invoice from Pixie Paper, are shown below.

Alpha Ltd

121 Baker St

Newcastle, NE1 7DJ

Purchase Order No. PO1792

To: Pixie Paper

Date: 5 Aug 20XX

Please supply 50 boxes of A4 paper product code 16257

Purchase price: £10 per box, plus VAT

Discount: less 10% trade discount, as agreed.

Pixie Paper

24 Eden Terrace, Durham, DH9 7TE

VAT Registration No. 464 392 401

Invoice No. 1679

Alpha Ltd

121 Baker St

Newcastle, NE1 7DJ

9 Aug 20XX

50 boxes of A4 paper, product code 16257 @ £10 each	£500
VAT	£100
Total	£600

Terms: 30 days net

Check the invoice against the purchase order and answer the following questions.

Has the correct product been supplied by Pixie Paper?	_Y_ / N
Has the correct net price been calculated?	_Y_ / N
Has the total invoice price been calculated correctly?	Y / _N_
What would be the VAT amount charged if the invoice was correct?	£ _90_
What would be the total amount charged if the invoice was correct?	£ _540_

60   ALPHA LTD

Shown below is a statement of account received from a credit supplier, and the supplier's account as shown in the purchases ledger of Alpha Ltd.

ABG Ltd

14 Hassle Street, Durham, DH9 7RQ

To: Alpha Ltd

121 Baker St

Newcastle, NE1 7DJ

STATEMENT OF ACCOUNT

Date 20XX	Invoice number	Details	Invoice amount £	Cheque amount £	Balance £
1 May	468	Goods	7,600		7,600
1 June		Cheque		2,500	5,100
5 June	472	Goods	4,200		9,300
12 June	478	Goods	500		9,800
22 June	486	Goods	1,680		11,480
30 June		Cheque		2,000	9,480

ABG Ltd

Date 20XX	Details	Amount £	Date 20XX	Details	Amount £
4 June	Bank	2,500	3 May	Purchases	7,600
28 June	Bank	2,000	8 June	Purchases	4,200
28 July	Purchase return	900	15 June	Purchases	500

(a)   Which item is missing from the statement of account from ABG Ltd?

> Purchase return 90

Picklist: Cheque for £2,500, invoice 468, Invoice 472, Purchase return £900, Invoice 486, Cheque for £2,000

(b)   Which item is missing from the supplier account in Alpha Ltd's purchases ledger?

> Invoice 486

Picklist: Invoice 468, Invoice 472, Invoice 478, Invoice 486, Purchase return £900, Cheque for £2,500

(c)   Once the omitted items have been recorded, what is the agreed balance outstanding between Alpha Ltd and ABG Ltd?

> 8580

61   MAXIMUS LTD

Alpha Ltd sends out cheques to suppliers on the last day of the month following the month of invoice. Below is an extract from the purchases ledger of Alpha Ltd.

Maximus Ltd

Date 20XX	Details	Amount £	Date 20XX	Details	Amount £
15 July	Purchases returns credit note 252	964	1 July	Balance b/f	5,980
21 July	Purchase return credit note 258	1,218	12 July	Purchases Invoice 864	6,386
31 July	Bank	5,980			

(a)   Complete the remittance advice note below.

Alpha Ltd

121 Baker St

Newcastle, NE1 7DJ

REMITTANCE ADVICE

To: Maximus Ltd 20XX   **Date:** 31 Aug

Please find attached our cheque in payment of the following amounts.

Invoice number	Credit note number	Amount £
Purchases Invoice 864		6,386
	Credit note # 252	964
	'' '' # 258	1,218
	Total amount paid	4,204

(b)   Are these two statements true or false?

A remittance note is for our records only   T / **F**

A remittance note is sent to a supplier to advise them of the amount being paid   **T** / F

62 HOLLY LTD

The account shown below is in the purchase ledger of AD Wholesale. A cheque for £4,770 has now been paid to this supplier.

Holly Ltd

Date 20XX	Details	Amount £	Date 20XX	Details	Amount £
			5 Jan	Balance b/f	1,500
15 Jan	Purchase return 251	540	19 Jan	Purchase invoice 3658	2,360
31 Jan	Purchase return 286	360	27 Jan	Purchase invoice 2987	1,450

(a) **Which item has been not been included in the payment, causing it to be overstated?**

Purchases returns 286

Picklist: Balance b/f, Purchase invoice 3658, Bank, Purchase returns 286, Purchase invoice 2987

An invoice has been received from Rickman Repairs for £860 plus VAT of £172. A prompt payment discount of 10% will be offered for payment within 30 days.

(b) **What is the amount we should pay, if we meet the 30 days requirement?**

£ 928.80

(c) **How much VAT is payable if the payment is NOT made in 30 days?**

£ 172

(d) **What is the amount we should pay if payment is NOT made within 30 days?**

£ 1,032

63   PAINTS R US

A supply of paint has been delivered to Painting Supplies Ltd by Paints R Us. The purchase order sent from Painting Supplies Ltd, and the invoice from Paints R Us, are shown below.

Painting Supplies Ltd

19 Edmund St

Newcastle, NE6 5DJ

Purchase Order No. PO6548

To: Paints R Us

Date: 5 Feb 20XX

Please supply 20 tins of blue paint, product code 23567

Purchase price: £8 per tin, plus VAT

Discount: less 5% prompt payment discount, as agreed.

Paints R Us

19 Valley Gardens, Stanley, DH5 8JJ

VAT Registration No. 421 385 602

Invoice No. 2485

Painting Supplies Ltd

19 Edmund St

Newcastle, NE6 5DJ

10 Feb 20XX

20 tins of blue paint, product code 23567 @ £8 each	£160.00
VAT	£30.00
Total	£190.00

Terms: 30 days net

Check the invoice against the purchase order and answer the following questions.

Has the correct product been supplied?	Y / N
Has the correct net price been calculated?	Y / N
Has the total invoice price been calculated correctly?	Y / N
What would be the VAT amount charged if the invoice was correct?	£ 32
What would be the total amount charged if the invoice was correct?	£ 192

64   EP MANUFACTURERS

Shown below is a statement of account received from a credit supplier, and the supplier's account as shown in the purchases ledger of EP Manufacturers.

KLP Ltd

19 Mussell Street, Newcastle, NE4 8JH

To: EP Manufacturers

19 Edmund St

Newcastle, NE6 5DJ

STATEMENT OF ACCOUNT

Date 20XX	Invoice number	Details	Invoice amount £	Cheque amount £	Balance £
1 Jan	468	Goods	5,200		5,200
3 Jan	458	Goods	3,600		8,800
8 Jan		Cheque		1,400	7,400
19 Jan	478	Goods	800		8,200
21 Jan		Cheque		6,500	1,700
28 Jan	488	Goods	4,350		6,050

KLP Ltd

Date 20XX	Details	Amount £	Date 20XX	Details	Amount £
8 Jan	Bank	1,400	1 Jan	Purchases	5,200
21 Jan	Bank	6,500	3 Jan	Purchases	3,600
31 Jan	Bank	1,200	19 Jan	Purchases	800

(a)   **Which item is missing from the statement of account from KLP Ltd?**

Cheque if £1,200

Picklist: Cheque for £1,200, invoice 468, Invoice 478, Cheque for £6,500, Invoice 488, Cheque for £1,400

(b)   **Which item is missing from the supplier account in EP Manufacturers' purchases ledger?**

Invoice 488

Picklist: Invoice 468, Invoice 472, Invoice 478, Invoice 488, Purchase return £900, Cheque for £2,500

(c)   **Once the omitted items have been recorded, what is the agreed balance outstanding between EP Manufacturers and KLP Ltd?**

£ 4,850

65   STANNY LTD

Ringo's Rings sends out cheques to suppliers on the last day of the month following the month of invoice. Below is an extract from the purchases ledger of Ringo's Rings.

Stanny Ltd

Date 20XX	Details	Amount £	Date 20XX	Details	Amount £
13 Feb	Purchases returns credit note 198	650	1 Feb	Balance b/f	4,650
19 Feb	Purchase return credit note 154	1,250	10 Feb	Purchases Invoice 694	2,300
28 Feb	Bank	4,650	11 Feb	Purchase invoice 658	3,640

(a)   Complete the remittance advice note below.

> **Ringo Rings**
>
> **37 Parker Lane**
>
> **Stoke SK1 0KE**
>
> **REMITTANCE ADVICE**
>
> **To:** Stanny Ltd   **Date:** 31 Mar 20XX
>
> Please find attached our cheque in payment of the following amounts.
>
> | Invoice number | Credit note number | Amount £ |
> |---|---|---|
> | Invoice 694 | | 2,300 |
> | 658 | | 3,640 |
> | | 198 | 650 |
> | | 154 | 1,250 |
> | | | |
> | **Total amount paid** | | 4,040 |

(b)   Are these two statements true or false?

A remittance note is for ours and the supplier's records   T / F

A remittance note is sent by a supplier confirming amounts received from them   T / F

66   TOYWORLD

Shown below is a statement of account received from a credit supplier, and the supplier's account as shown in the purchases ledger of Hickory House

Toyworld

18 Landview Road

Skipton

BD27 4TU

To: Hickory House

22 Nursery Road

Keighley, BD22 7BD

STATEMENT OF ACCOUNT

Date 20XX	Invoice number	Details	Invoice amount £	Cheque amount £	Balance £
1 Jan	207	Goods	2,500		2,500
8 April	310	Goods	900		3,400
9 June		Cheque		3,400	0
17 Aug	504	Goods	500		500
18 Aug	505	Goods	4,000		4,500

Toyworld

Date 20XX	Details	Amount £	Date 20XX	Details	Amount £
9 June	Bank	3,400	1 Jan	Purchases	2,500
25 June	Bank	500	8 April	Purchases	900
			17 Aug	Purchases	500

(a)   **Which item is missing from the statement of account from Toyworld?**

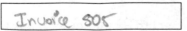

Cheque £500

Picklist: Invoice 207, Invoice 310, Invoice 504, Invoice 505, Cheque for £3,400, Cheque for £500

(b)   **Which item is missing from the supplier account in Hickory Houses' purchases ledger?**

Invoice 505

Picklist: Invoice 207, Invoice 310, Invoice 504, Invoice 505, Cheque for £3,400, Cheque for £500

(c)   **Assuming any differences between the statement of account from Toyworld and the supplier account in Hickory Houses' purchases ledger are simply due to omission errors, what is the amount owing to Toyworld?**

£   4000

67   HENRY HOUSE

Henry House sends out cheques to suppliers on the last day of the month following the month of invoice. Below is an extract from the purchases ledger of Henry House.

Abbies Party Ltd

Date 20XX	Details	Amount £	Date 20XX	Details	Amount £
17 July	Purchases returns credit note 27	82	15 July	Purchases Invoice 242	220
			10 Aug	Purchases Invoice 764	44

(a)   **Complete the remittance advice note below.**

Henry House

22 Nursery Road

Keighley, BD22 7BD

REMITTANCE ADVICE

To: Abbies Party

Date: 31 August 20XX

Please find attached our cheque in payment of the following amounts.

Invoice number	Credit note number	Amount £
242		220
764		44
	27	82
	Total amount paid	182

(b)   **Which of the following statements is true?**

A   The remittance advice note will be sent to the Inventory Dept to advise them inventory has been paid for

B   The remittance advice note will be sent to the customer to advise them of the amount being paid

C   The remittance advice note will be sent to Henry House's bank to confirm payment is to be made

D   The remittance advice note will be sent to the supplier to advise them of the amount being paid

68   GREY GARAGES

Grey Garages makes payments to suppliers by BACS on the 25th of every month and includes all items that have been outstanding for more than 10 days.

Below is a pre-printed remittance advice slip taken from a statement of account received from a supplier, Mulberry Motors, showing all items outstanding.

Complete the remittance advice ready for the next payment to Mulberry Motors.

Remittance advice			
To: Mulberry Motors			
From: Grey Garages			
Payment method: by Bacs		**Date of payment:** 25th of every month	
Items outstanding			
Date 20XX	**Details**	**Amount** £	**Tick if included in payment**
23-Jun	Invoice 213	740	✔
06-Jul	Credit note 14	120	✔
13-Jul	Invoice 216	620	✔
19-Jul	Invoice 257	870	
	Total amount paid		£ 1,240

69   ERRICO

The two invoices below were received on 5 June from credit suppliers who offer prompt payment discounts.

Invoices:

Giacomo
VAT registration 446 1552 01
Invoice number 1923

To: Errico	4 June 20XX
	£
4 product code 45 @ £14.50 each	58.00
VAT @ 20%	11.60
	———
Total	69.60

Terms: 3% prompt payment discount if payment is received within 7 days of the invoice date.

56.26
11.25

Gaetani
VAT registration 446 4742 01
Invoice number 4578

To: Errico	4 June 20XX
	£
3 product code 42a @ £11.50 each	34.50
VAT @ 20%	6.90
	———
Total	41.40

Terms: 5% prompt payment discount if payment is received within 5 days of the invoice date.

+.72
37.77
6.55

Calculate the amount to be paid to each supplier if the prompt payment discount is taken and show the date by which the supplier should receive the payment.

Supplier	£	Date by which the payment should be received by the supplier
Giacomo	*67.51*	*11 June 20XX*
Gaetani	*39.33*	*9 June 20XX*

70 MT MOTORS

MT Motors purchased goods costing £500 from Z (before VAT at 20%). Z gave MT Motors a trade discount of 20%.

(a) **What was the net amount to be recognised as a purchase expense after the discount?**

    A   £480.00

    B   £400.00

    C   £600.00

    D   £333.33

(b) **What was the VAT on purchases after trade discount?**

    A   £100.00

    B   £80.00

    C   £20.00

    D   £94.00

(c) **Which one of the following statements best describes the purpose of a purchase order?**

    A   It is issued to a supplier to request supply of goods from them on terms specified within the order.

    B   It is issued to a customer to confirm the supply of goods to them on terms specified in the order.

    C   It is issued to a supplier as notification of payment.

    D   It confirms the price that will be charged by a supplier for goods supplied.

DOCUMENTATION AND RECORDS FOR CUSTOMERS

71   ALESSANDRO LTD

On 1 Aug Alessandro Ltd delivered the following goods to a credit customer, Palermo Wholesale.

Alessandro Ltd
8 Alan Street
Glasgow, G1 7DJ

Delivery note No. 24369
01 Aug 20XX

Palermo Wholesale   **Customer account code:** AGG42
17 Zoo Lane
Dartford
DH8 4TJ

40 standard baths, product code SB05

The list price of the goods was £62.50 each plus VAT. Palermo Wholesale are to be given a 12% trade discount and a 5% discount if they pay within 5 working days.

(a)   Complete the invoice below.

Alessandro Ltd
8 Alan Street
Glasgow, G1 7DJ
VAT Registration No. 398 2774 01

Palermo Wholesale   **Customer account code:**
167 Front St
Stanley
DH8 4TJ   **Delivery note number:**
                                           Date: 1 Aug 20XX
Invoice No: 327

Quantity	Product code	Total list price £	Net amount after discount £	VAT £	Gross £
40	SB05	2,500	2,200	440	2,640

Alessandro Ltd offers each customer a discount of 5% if they pay within 30 days.

(b)   What is the name of this type of discount?

prompt payment d.

Picklist: Bulk discount, prompt payment discount, trade discount

72   HLB WHOLESALE

On 1 Feb Painting Supplies Ltd delivered the following goods to a credit customer, HLB Wholesale.

Painting Supplies Ltd	
19 Edmund St	
Newcastle, NE6 5DJ	

Delivery note No. 46589

01 Feb 20XX

HLB Wholesale   **Customer account code:** HLB24

98 Back St

Consett

DH4 3PD

20 tins of white paint, product code SD19

The list price of the goods was £15 each plus VAT. HLB Wholesale are to be given a 10% trade discount and a 4% discount if they pay within 4 working days.

(a)   Complete the invoice below.

Painting Supplies Ltd

19 Edmund St

Newcastle, NE6 5DJ

VAT Registration No. 402 2958 02

HLB Wholesale   **Customer account code:**

98 Back St

Consett

DH4 3PD   **Delivery note number:**

Date: 1 Feb 20XX   **Invoice No:** 298

Quantity	Product code	Total list price £	Net amount after discount £	VAT £	Gross £
20	SD19	300	270	54	324

Painting Supplies Ltd offer a discount of 10% if their customers buy from them.

(b)   What is the name of this type of discount?

trade discount

Picklist: Bulk discount, prompt payment discount, trade discount

73   MASHED LTD

On 1 Aug Hickory House delivered the following goods to a credit customer, Mashed Ltd.

Hickory House
22 Nursery Road
Keighley, BD22 7BD

Delivery note No. 472
01 Aug 20XX

Mashed Ltd   **Customer account code:** MA87
42 Moorside Court
Ilkley
Leeds, LS29 4PR

20 flower pots, product code P10

The list price of the goods was £5 per flower pot plus VAT. Mashed Ltd is to be given a 10% trade discount and a 4% early payment discount.

(a)   Complete the invoice below.

Hickory House
22 Nursery Road
Keighley, BD22 7BD

VAT Registration No. 476 1397 02

Mashed Ltd   **Customer account code:**
42 Moorside Court
Ilkley   **Delivery note number:**
Leeds, LS29 4PR

                                                                     Date: 1 Aug 20XX
Invoice No: 47

Quantity of pots	Product code	Total list price £	Net amount after discount £	VAT £	Gross £
20	P10	100	90	18	108

Hickory House offers each customer a discount if they buy over a certain quantity of goods.

(b)   What is the name of this type of discount?

Bulk discount

Picklist: Bulk discount, prompt payment discount, trade discount

74   WILLIAM & SAMMY LTD

The account shown below is in the sales ledger of Hickory House. A cheque for £668 has now been received from this customer.

William and Sammy Ltd

Date 20XX	Details	Amount £	Date 20XX	Details	Amount £
1 June	Balance b/f	4,250	2 June	Bank	4,250
23 June	Sales invoice 255	1,876	15 June	Sales returns credit note 98	1,208
30 June	Sales Invoice 286	2,459			

(a)   Which item has not been included in the payment?

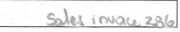

Sales invoice 286

Picklist: Balance b/f, Sales invoice 255, Sales invoice 286, Bank, Sales returns credit note 98

An invoice is being prepared to be sent to William and Sammy Ltd for £3,890 plus VAT of £778. A prompt payment discount of 4% will be offered for payment within 10 days.

155.6.
746.78
3734.4

(b)   What is the amount Hickory House should receive if payment is made within 10 days?

£ 4,431.28

(c)   What is the amount Hickory House should receive if payment is NOT made within 10 days?

£ 4,668

75   DIAMONDS & RUBIES LTD

The following is a summary of transactions with Diamonds & Rubies Ltd, a new credit customer.

Invoice 3927, 5 Aug. £4,640

Credit note 96, 10 Aug, £980

Invoice 3964, 21 Aug, £1,560

Credit note 104, 28 Aug, £650

Cheque received, 30 Aug, £2,100

Complete the statement of account below.

Stavros			
121 Baker St			
Newcastle, NE1 7DJ			
To: Diamonds & Rubies Ltd			**Date:** 31 Aug 20XX

Date 20XX	Details	Transaction amount £	Outstanding amount £
5 Aug	Invoice 3927	4640	4,640
10 Aug	Credit note 96	980	3,660
21 Aug	Invoice 3964	1560	5,220
28 Aug	Credit note 104	650	4,570
30 Aug	Cheque received	2,100	2,470

76 MAX LTD

The following is a summary of transactions with Max Ltd, a new credit customer of Painting Supplies Ltd.

Invoice 4658, 5 Feb. £2,560
Invoice 3964, 11 Feb, £3,290
Credit note 125, 21 Feb, £230
Credit note 139, 23 Feb, £560
Cheque received, 27 Feb, £1,900

Complete the statement of account below.

Painting Supplies Ltd			
19 Edmund St			
Newcastle, NE6 5DJ			
To: Max Ltd			**Date:** 28 Feb 20XX

Date 20XX	Details	Transaction amount £	Outstanding amount £
5 Feb	Invoice 4658	2,560	2,560
11 Feb	Invoice 3964	3,290	5,850
21 Feb	Credit note 125	230	5,620
23 Feb	Credit note 139	560	5,060
27 Feb	Cheque received	1,900	3,160

77   BETA BOARDS

The following is a summary of transactions with Ava Ltd, a new credit customer of Beta Boards

£350 re invoice 222 of 10 Aug

Cheque for £225 received 12 Aug

£744 re invoice 305 of 15 Aug

£339 re credit note 194 on 20 Aug

Cheque for £530 received 24 Aug

Complete the statement of account below.

Beta Boards

3 Victoria Avenue

Troon

KA5 2BD

To: Ava Ltd   **Date:** 31 Aug 20XX

Date 20XX	Details	Transaction amount £	Outstanding amount £
10 Aug	Invoice 222	350	350
12 Aug	Cheque	225	125
15 Aug	Invoice 305	744	869
20 Aug	Credit note 194	339	530
24 Aug	Cheque	530	0

UNDERSTANDING THE DOUBLE ENTRY SYSTEM

78   ACCOUNTING EQUATION

Financial accounting is based upon the accounting equation.

(a)   **Show whether the following statements are true or false.**

Assets less capital is equal to liabilities   _T_ / F

Assets plus liabilities are equal to capital   T / Ⓕ

Capital plus liabilities are equal to assets   _T_ / F

(b)   **Classify each of the following items as an asset or a liability by using the drop down lists.**

Item	Asset or liability?
Inventory	A
Machinery	A
5 year loan	L

79   CLASSIFICATION

Classify each of the accounts below by adjoining a line between the account and correct classification.

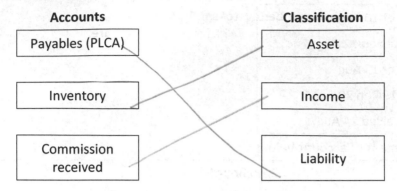

Accounts	Classification
Payables (PLCA)	Asset
Inventory	Income
Commission received	Liability

80   FINANCIAL ACCOUNTING

Financial accounting is based upon the accounting equation.

(a)   **Show whether the following statements are true or false.**

Capital is equal to assets plus liabilities   T / **F**

Assets less liabilities are equal to capital   **T** / F

Liabilities are equal to capital plus assets   T / **F**

(b)   **Classify each of the following items as an asset or a liability.**

Item	Asset or liability?
VAT owed to tax authorities	L
Amounts owing to payables	A̶ L
Money in the bank	A

81   CAPEX

It is important to understand the difference between capital expenditure, revenue expenditure, capital income and revenue income.

Select one option in each instance below to show whether the item will be capital income, revenue income, capital expenditure or revenue expenditure.

Item	Capital income	Revenue income	Capital expenditure	Revenue expenditure
Receipt from sale of motor vehicle	✓			
Receipts from credit sales		✓		
Purchase of machinery			✓	
Payment of electricity bill				✓
Purchase of goods for resale	⤫ (✓)			✓

82   REVEX

It is important to understand the difference between capital expenditure, revenue expenditure, capital income and revenue income.

Select one option in each instance below to show whether the item will be capital income, revenue income, capital expenditure or revenue expenditure.

Item	Capital income	Revenue income	Capital expenditure	Revenue expenditure
Receipt from sale of machinery	✓			
Payment of telephone bill				✓
Purchase of building			✓	
Receipts from cash sales	✗ (✓)	✓		
Receipts from receivables		✓		

83   EXPENDITURE TYPES

It is important to understand the difference between capital expenditure, revenue expenditure, capital income and revenue income.

Select one option in each instance below to show whether the item will be capital expenditure, revenue expenditure, capital income or revenue income.

Item	Capital expenditure	Revenue expenditure	Capital income	Revenue Income
Purchase of a new computer system	✓	✓ ✗		
Receipts from customers				✓
Receipt from sale of fixtures and fittings			✓	
Payments of salaries to staff		✓		
Purchase of cleaning materials		✓		
Receipt of bank interest	✓ ✗			✓

84   ASSET OR LIABILITY

(a)   Classify each of the following items as an asset or a liability by using the drop down lists.

Item	Asset or liability?
Factory building	A
Money due to suppliers	L
Car used in business	A

ABC Co has paid an electricity bill by cheque.

(b) **Complete the sentence below by selecting the correct option to show how this transaction will affect the accounts of ABC Co.**

The expense electricity will *increase* / *decrease*; the asset of bank will *increase* / *decrease*.

85 ACCOUNTING EQUATION 2

Show the accounting equation by inserting the appropriate figures using the information provided below:

Note: All figures should be shown as a positive balance.

Assets and liabilities	£
Land & buildings A	120,000
Cars & machinery A	20,960
Amounts due from credit customers A	4,900
Bank A	12,500
Amounts due to credit suppliers L	13,870
Loan L	15,000

Assets £	Liabilities £	Capital £
158,360	28,870	129,490

86 MULTIPLE CHOICE 1

(a) **State whether each of the following costs should be treated as capital expense or revenue expense.**

		Capital expense or revenue expense
(i)	Work to install additional, high-specification, electrical power cabling and circuits so that additional plant and equipment can become operational	capital expense
(ii)	Replacement of some loose and damaged roof tiles following a recent storm	revenue expense
(iii)	Repainting the factory administration office	revenue expense
(iv)	Modifications to the factory entrance to enable a large item of plant and equipment to be installed	capital expense

(b) **Which of the following statements best defines a statement of financial position?**

A It is a summary of income and expenditure for an accounting period

B It is a summary of cash receipts and payments made during an accounting period

C It is a summary of assets, liabilities and equity at a specified date

D It is a summary of assets and expenses at a specified date

(c) **The double-entry system of bookkeeping normally results in which of the following balances on the ledger accounts?**

	Debit balances:	Credit balances:
A	Assets and revenues	Liabilities, capital and expenses
B	Revenues, capital and liabilities	Assets and expenses
C	Assets and expenses	Liabilities, capital and revenues
D	Assets, expenses and capital	Liabilities and revenues

87 MULTIPLE CHOICE 2

(a) **Which of the following statements best defines a statement of profit or loss?**

A It is a summary of assets and expenses at a specified date

B It is a summary of cash receipts and payments made during an accounting period

C It is a summary of assets, liabilities and equity at a specified date

D It is a summary of income and expenditure for an accounting period

(b) **Which one of the following statements is correct?**

A Assets and liabilities normally have credit balances

B Liabilities and revenues normally have debit balances

C Assets and revenues normally have credit balances

D Assets and expenses normally have debit balances

(c) **Which one of the following statements is not correct?**

A A credit balance exists where the total of credit entries is more than the total of debit entries

B A debit balance exists where the total of debit entries is less than the total of credit entries

C A credit balance exists where the total of debit entries is less than the total of credit entries

D A debit balance exists where the total of debit entries is more than the total of credit entries

88   LEO

(a)   **Given below are a number of Leo's transactions. For each transaction, tick the relevant box to indicate whether it is a cash transaction or a credit transaction.**

TRANSACTION		CASH	CREDIT
(i)	Receipt of goods worth £140.59 from a supplier together with an invoice for that amount.	✓	✓
(ii)	Payment of £278.50 by cheque for a purchase at the till.	✓	
(iii)	Receipt of a deposit of £15.00 for goods.	✓	
(iv)	Sending of an invoice for £135.00 to the payer of the deposit for the remaining value of the goods.		✓
(v)	Sale of goods for £14.83, payment received by credit card.	✓	✓

(b)   **Given below are a number of typical transactions and balances that might be found in a business such as that run by Leo. Fill in the boxes to indicate whether the items are assets, liabilities, expenses or income.**

(i)	Goods stored in the warehouse awaiting resale	Asset
(ii)	Electricity bill paid	Expense
(iii)	Sale of goods	Income
(iv)	Amounts owing from a customer	Asset
(v)	Rent paid for the factory building	Expense
(vi)	Amounts due to the owner	Liability
(vii)	Amounts owed to suppliers	Liability
(viii)	Cash held in the till	Asset
(ix)	Machinery purchased for use in the factory	Asset
(x)	Rent received for subletting part of the factory premises	Income
(xi)	Cash held in the business bank account	Asset

Section 2

ANSWERS TO PRACTICE QUESTIONS

MAKING ENTRIES IN DAY BOOKS

1 SDB

Sales day-book

Date 20XX	Details	Invoice number	Total £	VAT £	Net £	Sales type 1 £	Sales type 2 £
31 Dec	Poonams	105	3,600	600	3,000		3,000
31 Dec	D. Taylor	106	7,680	1,280	6,400	6,400	
31 Dec	Smiths	107	3,840	640	3,200		3,200
	Totals		15,120	2,520	12,600	6,400	6,200

2 FREDDIE LTD

Purchases day-book

Date 20XX	Details	Invoice number	Total £	VAT £	Net £	Product 14211 £	Product 14212 £
31 July	Box Ltd	2177	960	160	800	800	
31 July	Shrew Ltd	2175	14,400	2,400	12,000	12,000	
31 July	Novot & Co	2176	4,800	800	4,000		4,000
	Totals		20,160	3,360	16,800	12,800	4,000

3 MAHINDRA LTD

Sales day-book

Date 20XX	Details	Invoice number	Total £	VAT £	Net £	Sales type 1 £	Sales type 2 £
31 Jan	Square Ltd	3567	1,200	200	1,000	1,000	
31 Jan	Oval & Co	3568	9,600	1,600	8,000		8,000
31 Jan	Diamond Ltd	3569	13,200	2,200	11,000		11,000
31 Jan	Triangle Ltd	3570	7,920	1,320	6,600	6,600	
	Totals		31,920	5,320	26,600	7,600	19,000

CODING

4 LEO LTD

(a) **Select which codes would be used to code this invoice.**

General ledger code	GL530
Customer account code	DEF14

(b) **Why is it useful to use a customer code?**

To help trace orders and amounts due from particular customers

5 ELLA'S PAINTS

(a) **Select which codes would be used to code this invoice.**

General ledger code	GL395
Supplier account code	MEG20

(b) **Why is it useful to use a supplier code?**

To help trace orders and amounts due to particular suppliers

6 ROBERTO & CO

(a) **Select which codes would be used to code this invoice.**

Supplier account code	ALE1
General ledger code	GL72

(b) **Why is it necessary to use a general ledger code?**

To help calculate expense incurred in a GL account

TRANSFERRING DATA FROM DAY BOOKS TO LEDGERS

7 LADY LTD

General ledger

Purchases ledger control account

	£		£
		1 Dec Balance b/d	5,103.90
		18 Dec Purchases & Vat	**903.23**

VAT account

	£		£
		1 Dec Balance b/d	526.90
18 Dec PLCA	**150.53**		

Purchases account

	£		£
1 Dec Balance b/d	22,379.52		
18 Dec PLCA	**752.70**		

Subsidiary ledger

M Brown

	£		£
		1 Dec Balance b/d	68.50
		1 Dec PDB	**300.00**

H Madden

	£		£
		1 Dec Balance b/d	286.97
		5 Dec PDB	**183.55**

L Singh

	£		£
		1 Dec Balance b/d	125.89
		7 Dec PDB	**132.60**

A Stevens

	£		£
		1 Dec Balance b/d	12.36
		10 Dec PDB	**90.00**

N Shema

	£		£
		1 Dec Balance b/d	168.70
		18 Dec PDB	**197.08**

8   BUTTONS LTD

(a)   What will be the entries in the purchases ledger?

Account name	Amount £	Debit ✓	Credit ✓
Peak & Co	6,240		✓
Max Ltd	12,720		✓
McIntyre Wholesale	5,760		✓
Pigmy Ltd	3,744		✓

(b)   What will be the entries in the general ledger?

Account name	Amount £	Debit ✓	Credit ✓
Purchases	23,720	✓	
VAT	4,744	✓	
Purchase ledger control	28,464		✓

9   SPARKY LTD

(a)   What will be the entries in the sales ledger?

Sales ledger

Account name	Amount £	Debit ✓	Credit ✓
Clarkson Ltd	1,680		✓
Kyle & Co	720		✓

(b)   What will be the entries in the general ledger?

General ledger

Account name	Amount £	Debit ✓	Credit ✓
Sales ledger control account	2,400		✓
Sales returns	2,000	✓	
VAT	400	✓	

10 LOUIS LTD

(a) **What will be the entries in the sales ledger?**

Account name	Amount £	Debit ✓	Credit ✓
Sheep & Co	3,840	✓	
Cow Ltd	11,760	✓	
Chicken & Partners	6,720	✓	
Pig Ltd	14,496	✓	

(b) **What will be the entries in the general ledger?**

Account name	Amount £	Debit ✓	Credit ✓
Sales ledger control	36,816	✓	
VAT	6,136		✓
Sales	30,680		✓

11 THOMAS & TILLY

(a) **What will be the entries in the purchases ledger?**

Purchase ledger

Account name	Amount £	Debit ✓	Credit ✓
May Ltd	1,920	✓	
Hammond & Co	1,200	✓	

(b) **What will be the entries in the general ledger?**

General ledger

Account name	Amount £	Debit ✓	Credit ✓
Purchase ledger control account	3,120	✓	
Purchase returns	2,600		✓
VAT	520		✓

12 FINCH'S

(a) **What will be the entries in the sales ledger?**

Account name	Amount £	Debit ✓	Credit ✓
Lou and Phil's	5,040	✓	
Eddie and Co	10,560	✓	
Noah's Arc	2,880	✓	
Alex and Freddie	720	✓	

(b)   **What will be the entries in the general ledger?**

Account name	Amount £	Debit ✓	Credit ✓
Sales	16,000		✓
VAT	3,200		✓
Sales ledger control	19,200	✓	

13   JESSICA & CO

(a)   **What will be the entries in the purchases ledger?**

Purchases ledger

Account name	Amount £	Debit ✓	Credit ✓
Iona Ltd	1,680	✓	
Matilda Ltd	4,320	✓	

(b)   **What will be the entries in the general ledger?**

General ledger

Account name	Amount £	Debit ✓	Credit ✓
Purchases ledger control account	6,000	✓	
Purchases returns	5,000		✓
VAT	1,000		✓

14   HORSEY REACH

(a)   **What will be the entries in the general ledger?**

Account name	Amount £	Debit ✓	Credit ✓
Sales ledger control	226.80		✓
VAT	37.80	✓	
Discounts allowed	189.00	✓	

(b)   **What will be the entries in the subsidiary ledger?**

Account name	Amount £	Debit ✓	Credit ✓
Ashleigh Buildings	36.00		✓
143 WGT	54.00		✓
McDuff McGregor	43.20		✓
Cameron Travel	93.60		✓

15 BUTTERFLY BEES

(a) **What will be the entries in the general ledger?**

Account name	Amount £	Debit ✓	Credit ✓
Discounts received	356.00		✓
VAT	71.20		✓
PLCA	427.20	✓	

(b) **What will be the entry in the purchases ledger?**

Account name	Amount £	Debit ✓	Credit ✓
Bella Bumps	24.00	✓	

16 OLIVIA ROSE BRIDAL SUPPLIES

(a) **What will be the entries in the general ledger?**

Account name	Amount £	Debit ✓	Credit ✓
Discounts allowed	189.00	✓	
VAT	37.80	✓	
SLCA	226.80		✓

(b) **What will be the entry in the sales ledger?**

Account name	Amount £	Debit ✓	Credit ✓
Bridezilla	54.00		✓

17 SUSSEX TRADING

(a) **What will be the entries in the general ledger?**

Account name	Amount £	Debit ✓	Credit ✓
Discounts allowed	410.00	✓	
VAT	82.00	✓	
SLCA	492.00		✓

(b) **What will be the entry in the sales ledger?**

Account name	Amount £	Debit ✓	Credit ✓
Woody Woodburn	78.00		✓

18 ROXY CAKE DESIGNS

(a) What will be the entries in the general ledger?

Account name	Amount £	Debit ✓	Credit ✓
Discounts allowed	318.00	✓	
VAT	63.60	✓	
SLCA	381.60		✓

(b) What will be the entry in the sales ledger?

Account name	Amount £	Debit ✓	Credit ✓
Percy Tran	33.60		✓

19 ANNANDALE SUPPLIES

(a) Show the correct entries to be made in the general ledger by entering the correct account name and debit or credit next to each amount.

Account name	Amount £	Debit/Credit
Purchases returns	4,580.00	Credit
VAT	916.00	Credit
Purchases ledger control	5,496.00	Debit

(b) Show the correct entries to be made in the general ledger by entering the correct account name and debit or credit next to each amount.

Account name	Amount £	Debit/Credit
Sales returns	2,501.00	Debit
VAT	500.20	Debit
Sales ledger control	3,001.20	Credit

20 NC CLEANING SUPPLIES

(a) Show the entries to be made in the general ledger by selecting the correct account name and debit or credit option against each amount. You may use each option more than once.

Account name	Amount £	Debit/Credit
Purchases ledger control	318.00	Debit
VAT	53.00	Credit
Purchases returns	265.00	Credit

(b)   Show the entries to be made in the general ledger by selecting the correct account name and debit or credit option against each amount. You may use each option more than once.

Account name	Amount £	Debit/Credit
Sales returns	150.00	Debit
VAT	30.00	Debit
Sales ledger control	180.00	Credit

THE CASH BOOK

21   ABC LTD

(a)   **Cash-book – Credit side**

Details	Cash	Bank	VAT	Payables	Cash purchases	Repairs and renewals
Balance b/f						
S. Lampard	216		36		180	
S. Bobbins	264		44		220	
Penny Rhodes	530				530	
Henley's Ltd		4,925		4,925		
Epic Equipment Maintenance		480	80			400
Total	1,010	5,405	160	4,925	930	400

(b)   **Cash book – Debit side**

Details	Cash	Bank	Receivables
Balance b/f	1,550	7,425	
D Davies		851	851
E Denholm		450	450
Total	1,550	8,726	1,301

(c)   Using your answers to (a) and (b) above calculate the cash balance.

£540

(d)   Using your answers to (a) and (b) above calculate the bank balance.

£3,321

(e)   Debit

22 BEDS

(a) **Cash-book – Credit side**

Details	Cash	Bank	VAT	Payables	Cash purchases	Repairs and renewals
Balance b/f						
A. Blighty Ltd	708		118		590	
R Bromby	228		38		190	
Roxy Bland	230				230	
Burgess Ltd		2,400		2,400		
Fast Equipment Repairs		96	16			80
Total	1,166	2,496	172	2,400	1,010	80

(b) **Cash book – Debit side**

Details	Cash	Bank	Receivables
Balance b/f	1,175	3,825	
A Barnett		698	698
H Connelly		250	250
Total	1,175	4,773	948

(c) **Using your answers to (a) and (b) above calculate the cash balance.**

£9

(d) **Using your answers to (a) and (b) above calculate the bank balance.**

£2,277

(e) **Will the bank balance calculated in (d) above be a debit or credit balance?**

Debit

23 JO'S

(a) **Cash-book – credit side**

Details	Cash	Bank	VAT	Payables	Cash purchases	Stationery expenses
Bal b/f		19,546				
T. Hunkin Ltd	48		8		40	
Victoria Green	96		16		80	
B. Head Ltd	455				455	
Smiths Ltd		4,250		4,250		
Arrow Valley Stationers		120	20			100
Total	599	23,916	44	4,250	575	100

(b) **Cash-book – debit side**

Details	Cash	Bank	Receivables
Balance b/f	986		
J Drummond		623	623
N Atkinson		425	425
Total	**986**	**1,048**	**1,048**

(c) **Using your answers to (a) and (b) above calculate the cash balance.**

£387

(d) **Using your answers to (a) and (b) above calculate the bank balance.**

£22,868

(e) **Will the bank balance calculated in (d) above be a debit or a credit balance?**

Credit

24 CHUGGER LTD

(a) **General ledger**

Account name	Amount £	Debit ✓	Credit ✓
Stationery expense	80	✓	
Repairs	200	✓	
VAT	56	✓	

(b) **Sales ledger**

Account name	Amount £	Debit ✓	Credit ✓
BBG Ltd	7,200		✓
EFG Ltd	5,000		✓

(c) **General ledger**

Account name	Amount £	Debit ✓	Credit ✓
Sales ledger control	12,200		✓

25 ITALIAN STALLIONS

(a) **General ledger**

Account name	Amount £	Debit ✓	Credit ✓
Office supplies	80	✓	
Repairs	160	✓	
VAT	48	✓	

(b) **Sales ledger**

Account name	Amount £	Debit ✓	Credit ✓
AAG Ltd	4,000		✓
HLG Ltd	3,000		✓

(c) **General ledger**

Account name	Amount £	Debit ✓	Credit ✓
Sales ledger control	7,000		✓

26 FRED'S FISH

(a) **Sales ledger**

Account name	Amount £	Debit ✓	Credit ✓
K and D Ltd	8,200		✓

(b) **General ledger**

Account name	Amount £	Debit ✓	Credit ✓
Sales ledger control	8,200		✓

(c) **General ledger**

Account name	Amount £	Debit ✓	Credit ✓
Stationery	100	✓	
VAT	20	✓	
Postage	800	✓	

PETTY CASH

27 HICKORY HOUSE

General ledger

Account name	Amount £	Debit ✓	Credit ✓
VAT	6.80	✓	
Postage	15.00	✓	
Motor expenses	12.40	✓	
Office expenses	21.60	✓	
Bank	90		✓

28 MESSI & CO

General ledger

Account name	Amount £	Debit ✓	Credit ✓
VAT	7.25	✓	
Postage	4.50	✓	
Motor expenses	8.00	✓	
Office expenses	28.28	✓	
Petty cash control	48.03		✓

29 STAVROS

General ledger

Account name	Amount £	Debit ✓	Credit ✓
VAT	18.86	✓	
Postage	16.00	✓	
Business travel	30.80	✓	
Sundry expenses	63.50	✓	
Bank	110.00		✓

30 YUMMY CUPCAKES

General ledger

Account name	Amount £	Debit ✓	Credit ✓
VAT	11.07	✓	
Sundry expenses	10.00	✓	
Business travel	45.37	✓	
Postage	4.00	✓	
Petty cash control	70.44		✓

31   OOH LA!

General ledger

Account name	Amount £	Debit ✓	Credit ✓
VAT	15.21	✓	
Postage	36.30	✓	
Sundry expenses	35.05	✓	
Motor expenses	17.00	✓	
Bank	70.00		✓

32   QUEEN VIC

(a)   **Reconcile the cash amount in the petty cash box with the balance on the petty cash account.**

Amount in petty cash box	**£141.00**
Balance on petty cash account	**£145.00**
Difference	**£4.00**

(b)   **Complete the petty cash reimbursement document below to restore the imprest amount of £150.**

Petty cash reimbursement	
Date: 31.07.20XX	
Amount required to restore the cash in the petty cash box.	**£122.75**

33   THE ARCHES

(a) – (b)

Petty cash-book

Debit side		Credit side					
Details	Amount £	Details	Amount £	VAT £	Postage £	Travel £	Stationery £
Balance b/f	200.00	Mick's Motors	20.00			20.00	
		Stamps	19.00		19.00		
		Office Essentials	26.40	4.40			22.00
		Balance c/d	134.60				
	200.00		200.00	4.40	19.00	20.00	22.00

34   RAINBOW

(a) – (b)

Petty cash-book

Debit side		Credit side					
Details	**Amount £**	**Details**	**Amount £**	**VAT £**	**Postage £**	**Travel £**	**Stationery £**
Balance b/f	100.00	Colin's Cabs	28.00			28.00	
		Post Office	18.00		18.00		
		ABC Stationery	38.40	6.40			32.00
		Balance c/d	15.60				
	100.00		**100.00**	**6.40**	**18.00**	**28.00**	**32.00**

35   SOOTY & SWEEP

(a)   **Reconcile the cash amount in the petty cash box with the balance on the petty cash account.**

Amount in petty cash box	**£127.40**
Balance on petty cash account	**£135.00**
Difference	**£7.60**

(b)   **Complete the petty cash reimbursement document below to restore the imprest amount of £250.**

Petty cash reimbursement	
Date: 31.07.20XX	
Amount required to restore the cash in the petty cash box.	**£245.00**

36 JAWS DENTISTRY

(a) – (b)

Petty cash-book

Debit side		Credit side					
Details	**Amount £**	**Details**	**Amount £**	**VAT £**	**Postage £**	**Travel £**	**Stationery £**
Balance b/f	225.00	Ace Taxis	26.00			26.00	
		Kate's Couriers	27.00		27.00		
		Smiths Stationery	45.60	7.60			38.00
		Balance c/d	126.40				
	225.00		**225.00**	**7.60**	**27.00**	**26.00**	**38.00**

37 TOM'S TILES

(a) Reconcile the cash amount in the petty cash box with the balance on the petty cash account.

Amount in petty cash box	**£162.12**
Balance on petty cash account	**£165.52**
Difference	**£3.40**

(b) Complete the petty cash reimbursement document below to restore the imprest amount of £250.00.

Petty cash reimbursement	
Date: 30.04.20XX	
Amount required to restore the cash in the petty cash box.	**£224.12**

38 ROCKY RILEY

(a) – (b)

Petty cash-book

Debit side		Credit side					
Details	Amount £	Details	Amount £	VAT £	Postage £	Travel £	Stationery £
Balance b/f	175.00	Kath's Kars	32.00			32.00	
		Stamps	25.00		25.00		
		Pauline's Pens	24.00	4.00			20.00
		Balance c/d	94.00				
	175.00		**175.00**	**4.00**	**25.00**	**32.00**	**20.00**

39 MHAIRI MOTORS

(a) **Reconcile the cash amount in the petty cash box with the balance on the petty cash account.**

Amount in petty cash box	**£99.80**
Balance on petty cash account	**£110.00**
Difference	**£10.20**

(b) **Complete the petty cash reimbursement document below to restore the imprest amount of £200.**

Petty cash reimbursement	
Date: 31.07.20XX	
Amount required to restore the cash in the petty cash box.	**£191.50**

40 DAINTY DESIGNS

(a) **Calculate the VAT and net amounts to be recorded in the petty cash book.**

VAT £	Net £
5.20	26.00

(b) **Calculate the total of the fuel expenses analysis column after the petty cash payment in (a) has been recorded.**

£91.66

(c)   What will be the entry in the petty cash book to record this transaction?

Details	Amount £	Debit ✓	Credit ✓
Cash from bank	237.70	✓	

(d)   What will be the entry in the petty cash book to record the closing balance on 31 March?

Details	Amount £	Debit ✓	Credit ✓
Balance c/d	280.00		✓

(e)   What will be the total, VAT and net amounts to be entered into the petty cash book?

Petty cash voucher	Total £	VAT £	Net £
222	32.40	5.40	27.00
223	12.00	2.00	10.00

41   JACKSON MOTORING

(a)   Calculate the VAT and net amounts to be recorded in the petty cash book.

VAT £	Net £
3.60	18.00

(b)   Calculate the total of the stationery expenses analysis column after the petty cash payment in (a) has been recorded.

£33.50

(c)   What will be the entry in the petty cash book to record this transaction?

Details	Amount £	Debit ✓	Credit ✓
Cash from bank	183.45	✓	

(d)   What will be the entry in the petty cash book to record the closing balance on 31 October?

Details	Amount £	Debit ✓	Credit ✓
Balance c/d	215.00		✓

(e)   What will be the total, VAT and net amounts to be entered into the petty cash book?

Petty cash voucher	Total £	VAT £	Net £
120	20.00	0	20.00
121	19.20	3.20	16.00

42   LJ INTERIORS

Account name	Amount £	Debit ✓	Credit ✓
VAT	64.00	✓	
Stationery	320.00	✓	
Postage	32.00	✓	
Charitable donations	150.00	✓	

43   KAZ KARATE CLUB

Account name	Amount £	Debit ✓	Credit ✓
VAT	31.00	✓	
Motor expenses	155.00	✓	
Postage	20.00	✓	
Insurance	180.00	✓	

44   JACINTA INTERIOR DESIGN

(a)   Complete the petty cash reimbursement document below to restore the imprest amount of £300.

Petty cash reimbursement	
Week 22	
Amount required to restore the cash in the petty cash box.	**£243.90**

	£
Stationery	42.30
Travelling cost	76.50
Refreshments	38.70
Sundry payables (£72.00 × (120/100)	86.40
	————
	243.90 to restore to £300
	————

(b)   Which one of the following states the entries required to account for the reimbursement to the petty cash float from the bank account?

A   Dr Petty cash   Cr Bank

45 MARTHA

(a) Calculate the VAT and net amounts of this petty cash payment to be recorded in the petty cash book.

VAT £	Net £
10.00	50.00

(b) Calculate the total of the cleaning expense analysis column after taking into consideration the petty cash payment in (a).

£62.40

(c) After taking into consideration the transaction in (a) what will be the entry in the petty cash book to restore to the imprest level of £150.

Details	Amount £	Debit ✓	Credit ✓
Cash from bank	117.36	✓	

(d) What is the entry made in the petty cash book to record the closing balance on 30th April?

Details	Amount £	Debit ✓	Credit ✓
Balance c/d	150.00		✓

(e) For each receipt identify the analysis column to be used for the payment and the amount of the transaction that should be recorded in the analysis column.

Petty cash receipt	Analysis column	Amount £
Newark Printers	Office expenses	14.50
ERJ Motor Supplies	Motor expenses	32.00
Co-pop	Cleaning expenses	5.00

DRAFTING AN INITIAL TRIAL BALANCE

46 BROOKLYN BOATS

(a) – (c)

Electricity

Date 20XX	Details	Amount £	Date 20XX	Details	Amount £
01 Dec	Balance b/f	870	31 Dec	Balance c/d	1,220
12 Dec	Bank	350			
	Total	1,220		Total	1,220
		1,220			

Discounts received

Date 20XX	Details	Amount £	Date 20XX	Details	Amount £
31 Dec	Balance c/d	600	1 Dec	Balance b/f	500
			15 Dec	Purchase Ledger control	100
	Total	600		Total	600
			1 Jan	Balance b/d	600

47 WIGGLE POGGLE LTD

(a) – (c)

Discount allowed

Date 20XX	Details	Amount £	Date 20XX	Details	Amount £
01 July	Balance b/f	1,560	31 July	Balance c/d	2,160
14 July	Sales ledger control account (SLCA)	480			
16 July	Sales ledger control account (SLCA)	120			
	Total	2,160		Total	2,160
1 Aug	Balance b/d	2,160			

Interest income

Date 20XX	Details	Amount £	Date 20XX	Details	Amount £
31 July	Balance c/d	400	01 July	Balance b/f	320
			28 July	Bank	80
	Total	400		Total	400
			1 Aug	Balance b/d	400

48   CRAZY CURTAINS

(a) – (c)

Electricity expense

Date 20XX	Details	Amount £	Date 20XX	Details	Amount £
01 Jan	Bal b/f	200	31 Jan	Balance c/d	450
22 Jan	Bank	250			
	Total	450		**Total**	450
1 Feb	Balance b/d	450			

Rental income

Date 20XX	Details	Amount £	Date 20XX	Details	Amount £
31 Jan	Balance c/d	1,000	01 Jan	Balance b/f	400
			28 Jan	Bank	600
	Total	1,000		**Total**	1,000
			1 Feb	Balance b/d	1,000

49   SMITH & SON

Account name	Amount £	Debit £	Credit £
Fixtures and fittings	8,250	8,250	
Capital	18,400		18,400
Bank overdraft	4,870		4,870
Petty cash control	350	350	
Sales ledger control (SLCA)	42,870	42,870	
Purchases ledger control (PLCA)	23,865		23,865
VAT owed to tax authorities	10,245		10,245
Inventory	9,870	9,870	
Loan from bank	22,484		22,484
Sales	180,264		180,264
Sales returns	5,420	5,420	
Purchases	129,030	129,030	
Purchases returns	2,678		2,678
Discount allowed	2,222	2,222	
Discount received	3,432		3,432
Heat and Light	1,490	1,490	
Motor expenses	2,354	2,354	
Wages	42,709	42,709	
Rent and rates	10,600	10,600	
Repairs	3,020	3,020	
Hotel expenses	1,890	1,890	
Telephone	2,220	2,220	
Delivery costs	1,276	1,276	
Miscellaneous expenses	2,667	2,667	
Totals	532,476	266,238	266,238

50 EXPIALIDOCIOUS LTD

Account name	Amount £	Debit £	Credit £
Capital	25,360		25,360
Petty cash control	250	250	
Loan from bank	11,600		11,600
Sales ledger control (SLCA)	159,242	159,242	
Purchases ledger control (PLCA)	83,682		83,682
Motor vehicles	35,900	35,900	
Inventory	28,460	28,460	
Bank overdraft	10,063		10,063
VAT owed from tax authorities	15,980	15,980	
Purchases	343,014	343,014	
Purchases returns	1,515		1,515
Wages	56,150	56,150	
Motor expenses	2,950	2,950	
Interest income	400		400
Sales	532,900		532,900
Sales returns	5,760	5,760	
Stationery	1,900	1,900	
Light & heat	6,500	6,500	
Discount received	200		200
Discount allowed	2,160	2,160	
Interest paid on overdraft	550	550	
Travel	1,800	1,800	
Marketing	650	650	
Telephone	1,510	1,510	
Miscellaneous expenses	2,944	2,944	
Totals		665,720	665,720

51   DIXON FURNITURE

Account name	Amount £	Debit £	Credit £
Motor vehicles	40,100	40,100	
Capital	35,000		35,000
Petty cash control	150	150	
Bank balance	14,654	14,654	
Wages	37,890	37,890	
Travel expenses	1,500	1,500	
Rental income	1,000		1,000
Sales	435,600		435,600
Loan from bank	10,000		10,000
Sales ledger control (SLCA)	127,456	127,456	
Inventory	22,500	22,500	
Purchases ledger control (PLCA)	91,250		91,250
VAT due to tax authorities	12,500		12,500
Purchases	325,600	325,600	
Sales returns	6,500	6,500	
Purchases returns	1,250		1,250
Sundry expenses	3,600	3,600	
Electricity expense	450	450	
Bank interest received	360		360
Fuel expense	900	900	
Discount received	600		600
Discount allowed	1,560	1,560	
Advertising	300	300	
Telephone	1,900	1,900	
Miscellaneous expenses	2,500	2,500	
Totals		587,560	587,560

52 BALANCES (1)

Account name	Balance c/d at 31 December £	Debit/Credit	Total shown in both the debit and credit columns £
Capital	6,000	Debit	6,000
Fixtures and Fittings	19,800	Credit	21,000
Loan	23,230	Debit	24,880
Drawings	2,450	Credit	2,450

53 BALANCES (2)

Account name	Balance c/d at 31 March £	Debit/Credit	Total shown in both the debit and credit columns £
Capital	15,000	Debit	15,000
Plant and Machinery	8,950	Credit	9,750
Loan	14,180	Debit	15,200
Drawings	4,220	Credit	4,220

54 ARCHIE

(a) Calculate the total of each of the debit and credit columns of the partially complete trial balance.

Debit £	Credit £
115,435	111,811

(b) Transfer each balance to the debit or credit column of the trial balance extract below.

Account name	Debit £	Credit £
Drawings	2,350	
Purchases ledger control		6,859
Discounts allowed	885	

(c) Calculate the final total to be entered into the debit and credit columns of the trial balance.

£118,670

(d) Identify SIX accounts that will appear in the trial balance and whether they will be transferred to the debit or credit column.

Account name	Debit	Credit	Does not appear in the trial balance
	✓	✓	✓
Fixtures and fittings	✓		
Capital		✓	
Discounts allowed	✓		
Rent received		✓	
Bank	✓		
Sales		✓	
Original Ltd			✓
Fvie & Joe			✓
Jacob & Danny			✓
PPR LLP			✓

55 HARRISON

(a) Calculate the total of each of the debit and credit columns of the partially complete trial balance.

Debit £	Credit £
109,155	113,390

(b) Transfer each balance to the debit or credit column of the trial balance extract below.

Account name	Debit £	Credit £
Drawings	8,000	
Capital		3,315
Discounts received		450

(c) Calculate the final total to be entered into the debit and credit columns of the trial balance.

£117,155

(d) Identify SIX accounts that will appear in the trial balance and whether they will be transferred to the debit or credit column

Account name	Debit ✓	Credit ✓	Does not appear in the trial balance ✓
Motor vehicles	✓		
Capital		✓	
Discounts received		✓	
Interest paid	✓		
Bank overdraft		✓	
Purchases	✓		
Dave & Malc Co			✓
Amy & Molly			✓
Peter & Paul			✓
Morris Ltd			✓

56 KOOKABURRA

(a) Calculate and insert the total of each of the debit and credit columns of the partially prepared trial balance.

Account name	Debit £	Credit £
Plant and equipment	106,340	
Sales ledger control (SLCA)	36,470	
Bank	12,590	
Inventory	18,240	
Purchases ledger control (PLCA)		27,021
Capital		50,000
Bank loan		2,590
Sales		625,640
Purchases	295,100	
Wages	32,410	
Administrative expenses	1,280	
Rent and rates	12,490	
Heat and light	4,291	
Entertainment expenses	456	
Telephone and broadband expenses	3,214	
Totals	522,881	705,251

(b)   Transfer each balance to the debit or credit column of the trial balance extract below.

Account name	Amount £	Debit £	Credit £
Purchases returns	14,980		14,980
Land and Buildings	197,000	197,000	
Petty cash	350	350	

(c)   Calculate the final total entered into the debit and credit columns of the trial balance.

£720,231

(d)   You are required to identify whether these accounts appear in the trial balance and if so whether they would be transferred to the debit or credit column.

Sales ledger

Account name	Account balance	Transfers to the trial balance in the DEBIT column	Transfers to the trial balance in the CREDIT column	Does not transfer to the trial balance
		✓	✓	✓
Riley Racing	£3,250			✓
Kat's Cakes	£2,560			✓

Purchases ledger

Account name	Account balance	Transfers to the trial balance in the DEBIT column	Transfers to the trial balance in the CREDIT column	Does not transfer to the trial balance
		✓	✓	✓
VK Supplies	£2,364			✓
TAF Ltd	£7,171			✓

General ledger

Account name	Account balance	Transfers to the trial balance in the DEBIT column	Transfers to the trial balance in the CREDIT column	Does not transfer to the trial balance
		✓	✓	✓
Sales returns	£23,910	✓		
Bank overdraft	£2,185		✓	

57 ALAN

(a) If Alan's trial balance balances, what is the missing figure for the sales ledger control?

B   £111,000

Working:

Account	Debit £	Credit £
Sales		628,000
Cost of sales	458,000	
General expenses	138,000	
Purchases ledger control		54,000
Sales ledger control (balancing figure)	111,000	
Bank (in funds)	61,000	
Capital		86,000
Totals	**768,000**	**768,000**

(b) Taking into consideration the answer to part (a) what is the trial balance total?

£768,000   See working in part (a).

(c) Which of the following balances would appear on the same side in the trial balance?

B   Assets, expenses and drawings are debit balances in the trial balance.

DOCUMENTATION AND RECORDS FOR SUPPLIERS

58 NAN NURSING

Has the correct purchase price of the chocolate puddings been charged on the invoice?	N
Has the correct discount been applied?	Y
What would be the VAT amount charged if the invoice was correct?	£18.00
What would be the total amount charged if the invoice was correct?	£108.00

59 PIXIE PAPERS

Has the correct product been supplied by Pixie Paper?	Y
Has the correct net price been calculated?	N see **N1**
Has the total invoice price been calculated correctly?	N
What would be the VAT amount charged if the invoice was correct?	£90.00
What would be the total amount charged if the invoice was correct?	£540.00

N1 – the trade discount of 10% should have been deducted so that the net price was £450.

VAT @ 20% on the net price of £450 is then calculated as £90.00.

60 ALPHA LTD

(a) **Which item is missing from the statement of account from ABG Ltd?**

| Purchase return £900 |

(b) **Which item is missing from the supplier account in Alpha Ltd's purchases ledger?**

| Invoice 486 |

(c) **Once the omitted items have been recorded, what is the agreed balance outstanding between Alpha Ltd and ABG Ltd?**

| £8,580.00 |

61 MAXIMUS LTD

(a) **Complete the remittance advice note below.**

Alpha Ltd

121 Baker St

Newcastle, NE1 7DJ

REMITTANCE ADVICE

To: Maximus Ltd 20XX   **Date:** 31 Aug

Please find attached our cheque in payment of the following amounts.

Invoice number	Credit note number	Amount £
864		6,386
	252	964
	258	1,218
	Total amount paid	4,204

(b) **Are these two statements true or false?**

A remittance note is for our records only	F
A remittance note is sent to a supplier to advise them of the amount being paid	T

62 HOLLY LTD

(a) Which item has been not been included in the payment, causing it to be overstated?

Purchase return 286

(b) What is the amount we should pay, if we meet the 30 days requirement?

£928.80

(c) How much VAT is payable if the payment is NOT made in 30 days?

£172.00

(d) What is the amount we should pay if payment is NOT made within 30 days?

£1,032.00

63 PAINTS R US

Has the correct product been supplied?	Y
Has the correct net price been calculated?	Y
Has the total invoice price been calculated correctly?	N
What would be the VAT amount charged if the invoice was correct?	£32.00
What would be the total amount charged if the invoice was correct?	£192.00

64 EP MANUFACTURERS

(a) Which item is missing from the statement of account from KLP Ltd?

Cheque for £1,200

(b) Which item is missing from the supplier account in EP Manufacturers' purchases ledger?

Invoice 488

(c) Once the omitted items have been recorded, what is the agreed balance outstanding between EP Manufacturers and KLP Ltd?

£4,850.00

65 STANNY LTD

(a) Complete the remittance advice note below.

Ringo Rings

37 Parker Lane

Stoke SK1 0KE

REMITTANCE ADVICE

To: Stanny Ltd   **Date:** 31 Mar 20XX

Please find attached our cheque in payment of the following amounts.

Invoice number	Credit note number	Amount £
694		2,300
658		3,640
	198	650
	154	1,250
	Total amount paid	4,040

(b) Are these two statements true or false?

A remittance note is for ours and the suppliers records	T
A remittance note is sent by a supplier confirming amounts received from them	F

66 TOYWORLD

(a) Which item is missing from the statement of account from Toyworld?

Cheque for £500

Picklist: Invoice 207, Invoice 310, Invoice 504, Invoice 505, Cheque for £3,400, Cheque for £500

(b) Which item is missing from the supplier account in Hickory Houses' purchases ledger?

Invoice 505

Picklist: Invoice 207, Invoice 310, Invoice 504, Invoice 505, Cheque for £3,400, Cheque for £500

(c) Assuming any differences between the statement of account from Toyworld and the supplier account in Hickory Houses' purchases ledger are simply due to omission errors, what is the amount owing to Toyworld?

£4,000

67   HENRY HOUSE

(a)   **Complete the remittance advice note below.**

Henry House

22 Nursery Road

Keighley, BD22 7BD

REMITTANCE ADVICE

To: Abbies Party

Date: 31 August 20XX

Please find attached our cheque in payment of the following amounts.

Invoice number	Credit note number	Amount £
242		220
	27	82
Total amount paid		138

(b)   **Which of the following statements is true?**

D   The remittance advice note will be sent to the supplier to advise them of the amount being paid

68   GREY GARAGES

		Remittance advice		
To: Mulberry Motors				
From: Grey Garages				
Payment method: BACS			**Date of payment:** 25 July	

Items outstanding			Tick if included in payment
Date 20XX	**Details**	**Amount** £	
23-Jun	Invoice 213	740	✓
06-Jul	Credit note 14	120	✓
13-Jul	Invoice 216	620	✓
19-Jul	Invoice 257	870	
Total amount paid			£1,240

69   ERRICO

Supplier	£	Date by which the payment should be received by the supplier
Giacomo	67.51	11 June 20XX
Gaetani	39.33	9 June 20XX

70   MT MOTORS

(a)   What was the net amount to be recognised as a purchase expense after the discount?

   B   £400.00

	£
List price	500
Less: Trade discount (20% × £500)	(100)
	———
Purchases	400
	———

(b) **What was the VAT on purchases after trade discount?**

B   £80.00

	£
List price	500.00
Less: Trade discount	(100.00)
Net purchases	400.00
VAT @ 20%	80.00
	480.00

(c)   **Which one of the following statements best describes the purpose of a purchase order?**

A   It is issued to a supplier to request supply of goods from them on terms specified within the order.

DOCUMENTATION AND RECORDS FOR CUSTOMERS

71   ALESSANDRO LTD

(a)   **Complete the invoice below.**

Alessandro Ltd
8 Alan Street
Glasgow, G1 7DJ
VAT Registration No. 398 2774 01

Palermo Wholesale
167 Front St
Stanley
DH8 4TJ

Customer account code: AGG42

Delivery note number: 24369
Date: 1 Aug 20XX

Invoice No: 327

Quantity	Product code	Total list price £	Net amount after discount £	VAT £	Gross £
40	SB05	2,500	2,200	440	2,640

(b)   **What is the name of this type of discount?**

Prompt payment discount

72   HLB WHOLESALE

(a)   **Complete the invoice below.**

Painting Supplies Ltd
19 Edmund St
Newcastle, NE6 5DJ

VAT Registration No. 402 2958 02

HLB Wholesale   **Customer account code:** HLB24
98 Back St
Consett
DH4 3PD   **Delivery note number: 46589**

Date: 1 Feb 20XX   **Invoice No:** 298

Quantity	Product code	Total list price £	Net amount after discount £	VAT £	Gross £
20	SD19	300	270	54	324

(b)   **What is the name of this type of discount?**

Trade discount

73   MASHED LTD

(a)   **Complete the invoice below.**

Hickory House
22 Nursery Road
Keighley, BD22 7BD

VAT Registration No. 476 1397 02

Mashed Ltd   **Customer account code:** MA87
42 Moorside Court
Ilkley   **Delivery note number: 472**
Leeds, LS29 4PR

                                                 Date: 1 Aug 20XX

Invoice No: 47

Quantity of pots	Product code	Total list price £	Net amount after discount £	VAT £	Gross £
20	P10	100	90	18	108

(b)   **What is the name of this type of discount?**

Bulk discount

74 WILLIAM & SAMMY LTD

(a) **Which item has not been included in the payment?**

Sales invoice 286

(b) **What is the amount Hickory House should receive if payment is made within 10 days?**

£4,481.28

(c) **What is the amount Hickory House should receive if payment is NOT made within 10 days?**

£4,668.00

75 DIAMONDS & RUBIES LTD

Stavros			
121 Baker St			
Newcastle, NE1 7DJ			
To: Diamonds & Rubies Ltd			**Date:** 31 Aug 20XX
Date 20XX	**Details**	**Transaction amount £**	**Outstanding amount £**
5 Aug	Invoice 3927	4,640	4,640
10 Aug	Credit note 96	980	3,660
21 Aug	Invoice 3964	1,560	5,220
28 Aug	Credit note 104	650	4,570
30 Aug	Cheque received	2,100	2,470

76 MAX LTD

Painting Supplies Ltd			
19 Edmund St			
Newcastle, NE6 5DJ			
To: Max Ltd			**Date:** 28 Feb 20XX
Date 20XX	**Details**	**Transaction amount £**	**Outstanding amount £**
5 Feb	Invoice 4658	2,560	2,560
11 Feb	Invoice 3964	3,290	5,850
21 Feb	Credit note 125	230	5,620
23 Feb	Credit note 139	560	5,060
27 Feb	Cheque received	1,900	3,160

77 BETA BOARDS

	Beta Boards		
	3 Victoria Avenue		
	Troon		
	KA5 2BD		
To: Ava Ltd		**Date:** 31 Aug 20XX	
Date 20XX	**Details**	**Transaction amount £**	**Outstanding amount £**
10 Aug	Invoice 222	350	350
12 Aug	Cheque	225	125
15 Aug	Invoice 305	744	869
20 Aug	Credit note 194	339	530
24 Aug	Cheque	530	0

UNDERSTANDING THE DOUBLE ENTRY SYSTEM

78 ACCOUNTING EQUATION

(a) **Show whether the following statements are true or false.**

Assets less capital is equal to liabilities	T
Assets plus liabilities are equal to capital	F
Capital plus liabilities are equal to assets	T

(b) **Classify each of the following items as an asset or a liability by using the drop down lists.**

Item	Asset or liability?
Inventory	Asset
Machinery	Asset
5 year loan	Liability

79 CLASSIFICATION

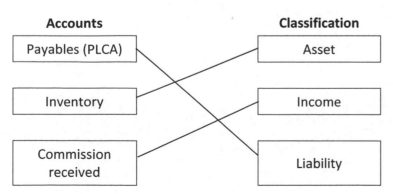

80 FINANCIAL ACCOUNTING

(a) Show whether the following statements are true or false.

Capital is equal to assets plus liabilities	F
Assets less liabilities are equal to capital	T
Liabilities are equal to capital plus assets	F

(b) Classify each of the following items as an asset or a liability.

Item	Asset or liability?
VAT owed to tax authorities	Liability
Amounts owing to payables	Liability
Money in the bank	Asset

81 CAPEX

Item	Capital income	Revenue income	Capital expenditure	Revenue expenditure
Receipt from sale of motor vehicle	✓			
Receipts from credit sales		✓		
Purchase of machinery			✓	
Payment of electricity bill				✓
Purchase of goods for resale				✓

82 REVEX

Item	Capital income	Revenue income	Capital expenditure	Revenue expenditure
Receipt from sale of machinery	✓			
Payment of telephone bill				✓
Purchase of building			✓	
Receipts from cash sales		✓		
Receipts from receivables		✓		

83 EXPENDITURE TYPES

Item	Capital expenditure	Revenue expenditure	Capital income	Revenue income
Purchase of a new computer system	✓			
Receipts from customers				✓
Receipt from sale of fixtures and fittings			✓	
Payments of salaries to staff		✓		
Purchase of cleaning materials		✓		
Receipt of bank interest				✓

84 ASSET OR LIABILITY

(a) Classify each of the following items as an asset or a liability by using the drop down lists.

Item	Asset or liability?
Factory building	Asset
Money due to suppliers	Liability
Car used in business	Asset

(b) Complete the sentence below by selecting the correct option to show how this transaction will affect the accounts of ABC Co.

The expense electricity will *increase*; the asset of bank will *decrease*.

85 ACCOUNTING EQUATION 2

Assets £	Liabilities £	Capital £
158,360	28,870	129,490

86 MULTIPLE CHOICE 1

(a)   State whether each of the following costs should be treated as capital expense or revenue expense.

		Capital expense or revenue expense
(i)	Work to install additional, high-specification, electrical power cabling and circuits so that additional plant and equipment can become operational	Capital
(ii)	Replacement of some loose and damaged roof tiles following a recent storm	Revenue
(iii)	Repainting the factory administration office	Revenue
(iv)	Modifications to the factory entrance to enable a large item of plant and equipment to be installed	Capital

(b)   **Which of the following statements best defines a statement of financial position?**

C   It is a summary of assets, liabilities and equity at a specified date

(c)   **The double-entry system of bookkeeping normally results in which of the following balances on the ledger accounts?**

Debit balances: *Credit balances:*

C   Assets and expenses   Liabilities, capital and revenues

87 MULTIPLE CHOICE 2

(a)   **Which of the following statements best defines a statement of profit or loss?**

D   It is a summary of income and expenditure for an accounting period

(b)   **Which one of the following statements is correct?**

D   Assets and expenses normally have debit balances

(c)   **Which one of the following statements is not correct?**

B   A debit balance exists where the total of debit entries is less than the total of credit entries

88 LEO

(a) Given below are a number of Leo's transactions. For each transaction, tick the relevant box to indicate whether it is a cash transaction or a credit transaction.

TRANSACTION	CASH	CREDIT
(i) Receipt of goods worth £140.59 from a supplier together with an invoice for that amount.		✓
(ii) Payment of £278.50 by cheque for a purchase at the till.	✓	
(iii) Receipt of a deposit of £15.00 for goods.	✓	
(iv) Sending of an invoice for £135.00 to the payer of the deposit for the remaining value of the goods.		✓
(v) Sale of goods for £14.83, payment received by credit card.	✓	

(b) Given below are a number of typical transactions and balances that might be found in a business such as that run by Leo. Fill in the boxes to indicate whether the items are assets, liabilities, expenses or income.

(i) Asset – inventory

(ii) Expense

(iii) Income

(iv) Asset – trade receivables

(v) Expense

(vi) Liability (this is a special liability known as capital)

(vii) Liability – payables

(viii) Asset

(ix) Asset

(x) Income

(xi) Asset

Section 3

MOCK ASSESSMENT QUESTIONS

TASK 1.1 (12 marks)

On 1 December Rocky Ricardo delivered the following goods to a credit customer, Alpha Group.

Rocky Ricardo
1 Rocky Way
Middleton, M42 5TU

Delivery note No. 2132
01 Dec 20XX

Alpha Group   **Customer account code:** ALP01
Alpha House
Warwick
WR11 5TB

200 cases of product A, product code A1.

The list price of the goods was £10 per case plus VAT. Alpha Group are to be given a 10% trade discount and a 2% prompt payment discount.

(a)   Complete the invoice below. (4 marks)

Rocky Ricardo
1 Rocky Way
Middleton, M42 5TU

VAT Registration No. 298 3827 04

Alpha Group   **Customer account code:**
Alpha House
Warwick   **Delivery note number:**
WR11 5TB
                                                       Date: 1 Dec 20XX
Invoice No: 950

Quantity of cases	Product code	Total list price £	Net amount after discount £	VAT £	Gross £
200	A1	2,000	1,800	360	2,160

(b) What will be the amounts entered into the sales day book after the invoice in (a) has been prepared? **(3 marks)**

Sales day book					
Date 20XX	Details	Invoice No:	Total £	VAT £	Net £
1 Dec	Alpha Group	950	2,160	360	2,800

(c) A cheque for £1,000 has now been received from Alpha Group which incorrectly states is full settlement of their account. Their account in the sales ledger is shown below:

Alpha Group

Date 20XX	Details	Amount £	Date 20XX	Details	Amount £
3 Oct	Bank	4,288	1 Oct	Balance b/f	4,288
25 Nov	Purchase returns credit note 102	500	21 Nov	Purchase invoice 123	1,500
			29 Nov	Purchase invoice 189	2,000

Which item has not been included in the payment? **(2 marks)**

Purchase Invoice 189

Select your account name from the following list: Balance b/f, Purchase invoice 123, Purchase invoice 189, Bank, Purchase returns credit note 102

(d) An invoice has been sent to Alpha Group for £500 plus VAT of £100. A prompt payment discount of 1% has been offered for payment within 5 days.

(i) What is the amount Alpha Group should pay if payment is made within 5 days? **(2 marks)**

£ 594

(ii) What is the amount Alpha Group should pay if payment is NOT made within 5 days? **(1 mark)**

£ 600

TASK 1.2 (9 marks)

A supply of cardboard boxes has been delivered to Rocky Ricardo's by Echo Ltd. The purchase order sent from Rocky Ricardo's, and the invoice from Echo Ltd, are shown below.

Rocky Ricardo

1 Rocky Way

Middleton, M42 5TU

Purchase Order No. RR111

To: Echo Ltd

Date: 7 Dec 20XX

Please supply 1,000 widgets product code 243

Purchase price: £1 per widget, plus VAT

Discount: less 10% trade discount, as agreed

Echo Ltd

2 Walford Way, Essex, ES4 4XX

VAT Registration No. 533 8372 12

Invoice No. 123

Rocky Ricardo

1 Rocky Way

Middleton, M42 5TU

10 Dec 20XX

1,000 .... widgets product code 243 @ £1 each	£1,000.00
VAT	£200.00
Total	£1,200.00

Terms: 30 days net

(a) **Check the invoice against the purchase order and answer the following questions.**

(4 marks)

Has the correct discount been applied?	Y / <u>N</u>
How much should the trade discount amount to?	£ 100
What would be the VAT amount charged if the invoice was correct?	£ 180

(b)   The following invoice has been received from the credit supplier Messi Brothers.

Messi Brothers
Unit 3 Fothersway Business Park, Newcastle
VAT Registration No. 933 8982 02
Invoice No. 1365

Rocky Ricardo
1 Rocky Way
Middleton, M42 5TU

10 Dec 20XX

500 .... of product code 1872 @ £3.75 each	£1,875.00
VAT	£375.00
Total	£2,250.00

Terms: 30 days net

What will be the details and amounts entered into the day book?   **(5 marks)**

Day book:

Date 20XX	Details	Invoice No:	Total £	VAT £	Net £
10 Dec	Rocky Ricardo	1365	2,250	375	1,875

TASK 1.3   (9 marks)

The two invoices below were received on 20 October from credit suppliers of Lewin & Co who offer prompt payment discounts.

Invoices:

Bridge Brothers
VAT registration 446 4752 01
Invoice number 193

To: Lewin & Co   19 October 20XX

	£
5 product code 895 @ £18.75 each	93.75
VAT @ 20%	18.75
Total	112.50

Terms: 2% prompt payment discount if payment is received within 4 days of the invoice date.

Mitchells

VAT registration 446 4742 01

Invoice number 578

To: Lewin & Co   19 October 20XX

	£
9 product code 756 @ £13.25 each	119.25
VAT @ 20%	23.85
	————
Total	143.10

Terms: 10% prompt payment discount if payment is received within 5 days of the invoice date.

(a) **Calculate the amount to be paid to each supplier if the prompt payment discount is taken and show the date by which the supplier should receive the payment.** **(4 marks)**

Supplier	£	Date by which the payment should be received by the supplier
Bridge Brothers	110,25	23-12-20XX
Mitchells	128,79	24-12-20XX

It is the policy of Lewin & Co to check each supplier statement as they arrive to ensure that they agree to the individual accounts within the purchases ledger. Provided below is the statement of account from Xcess Stock and their account in the purchases ledger.

Lewin & Co's policy is to only pay for items from the supplier statement which appear in their account in the purchases ledger.

(b) **Place a tick next to the 3 items in the supplier statement which will not be included within the payment.** **(3 marks)**

Date 20XX	Details	Amount £	Date 20XX	Details	Amount £
21 Dec	Credit note 101	940	12 Dec	Invoice 1001	1,700
			21 Dec	Invoice 1004	2,350
31 Dec	Balance c/d	3,580	27 Dec	Invoice 1010	470
		4,520			4,520
			20XY 1 Jan	Balance b/d	3,580

	Xcess Stock		
	Unit 7 Windy Industrial Estate		Not to be paid
	Irvine, KA6 8HU		
To: Lewin & Co			
Date: 31 Dec 20XX			

Date 20XX	Details	Transaction amount £	
12 Dec	Invoice 1001	1,700	
13 Dec	Invoice 1003	1,500	✓
21 Dec	Invoice 1004	2,350	
21 Dec	Credit note 101	940	
22 Dec	Invoice 1005	450	✓
27 Dec	Invoice 1010	470	
28 Dec	Credit note 102	50	✓

(c) **What will be the amount paid to Xcess Stock by Lewin & Co? (1 mark)**

£   7,460

(d) One of the accounts within the purchases ledger of Lewin & Co is for the credit supplier Minto Madness. A credit note for a prompt payment discount of £20 plus VAT has been received from Minto Madness. Before processing the credit note, the balance on the account of Minto Madness is £1,540.

What is the amount remaining on the account taking into consideration the credit note?

(1 mark)

£   1,516

TASK 1.4   (15 marks)

There are five payments to be entered in Carter's cash-book.

Receipts

Received cash with thanks for goods bought.	Received cash with thanks for goods bought.
From Carter's, a customer without a credit account.	From Carter's, a customer without a credit account.
Net £800	Net £200
VAT £160	VAT £40
Total £960	Total £240
J Pumpkin	*B Row*

Cheque book counterfoils

Lemon Ltd	Remo Motor	Fencer
(Purchase ledger account LEM002)	(no credit account)	(Purchase ledger account FEN001)
£100	£240 including VAT	£600
000123	000124	000125

(a) Enter the details from the two receipts and three cheque book stubs into the credit side of the cash-book shown below and total each column. (6 marks)

Cash book – Credit side

Details	Cash	Bank	VAT	Payables	Cash purchases	Motor expenses
Balance b/f		11,450				
J Pumpkin	960		160		800	
B Row	240		40		200	
Lemon Ltd		100		100		
Remo Motor		240	40			200
Fencer		600		600		
Total	1,200	12,390	240	700	1,000	200

There are two cheques from credit customers to be entered in Carter's cash book:

Jeff Jolly £127

Dolly Darton £310

(b) Enter the above details into the debit side of the cash-book and total each column. (4 marks)

Cash book – Debit side

Details	Cash	Bank	Receivables
Balance b/f	1,850		
Jeff Jolly		127	127
Dolly Darton		310	310
Total	1,850	437	437

(c) Using your answers to (a) and (b) above, calculate the cash balance. (2 marks)

£ 650

(d) Using your answers to (a) and (b) above, calculate the bank balance. (2 marks)

£ 11,953

(e) Will the bank balance calculated in (d) above be a debit or credit balance? (1 mark)

Debit/Credit

TASK 1.5 (15 marks)

A business maintains a petty cash book as both a book of prime entry and part of the double entry accounting system. The petty cash book below has been partly completed for the month of June.

Petty cash-book

Date 20XX	Details	Amount £	Date 20XX	Details	Amount £	VAT £	Motor expenses £	Cleaning expenses £	Office expenses £
01 Jun	Bank	200.00	15 Jun	Fuel	38.40	6.40	32.00		
			17 Jun	Office Supplies Ltd	24.00	4.00			20.00

On 30th June there was one final petty cash payment for the month to be recorded:

Office Supplies Ltd £72 including VAT

(a) Calculate the VAT and net amounts of this petty cash payment to be recorded in the petty cash book. **(2 marks)**

VAT £	Net £
12	60

(b) Calculate the total of the office expense analysis column after taking into consideration the petty cash payment in (a). **(1 mark)**

£ 80

(c) After taking into consideration the transaction in (a) what will be the entry in the petty cash book to restore to the imprest level of £200. **(3 marks)**

Details	Amount £	Debit ✓	Credit ✓
Cash from Bank	134.40	✓	

Details picklist: Amount, Balance b/d, Balance c/d, Cash from bank

(d) What is the entry made in the petty cash book to record the closing balance on 30th June? **(3 marks)**

Details	Amount £	Debit ✓	Credit ✓
Balance c/d	200		✓

Details picklist: Amount, Balance b/d, Balance c/d, Cash from bank

The following petty cash receipts need to be recorded in the petty cash book for the month of July.

177	178	179
Printing Partners	**Annan Motor Supplies**	**Your Local Convenience**
Printer ink	Engine oil	Washing up liquid & dish cloths
£49.38 including VAT of £8.23.	£14.50 plus VAT of £2.90.	£5.60 net of £1.12 VAT.

(e) For each receipt identify the analysis column to be used for the payment and the amount of the transaction that should be recorded in the analysis column. **(6 marks)**

Petty cash receipt	Analysis column	Amount £
Printing Partners	Office expenses	41.15
Annan Motor Supplies	Motor expenses	14.50
Your Local Convenience	Cleaning expenses	5.60

Analysis column picklist: Cleaning expenses, Motor expenses, Office expenses

TASK 1.6 (12 marks)

The following transactions all took place on 31 July and have been entered into the discounts allowed day book of Roland's as shown below. No entries have yet been made into the ledger system.

Date 20XX	Details	Credit note number	Total £	VAT £	Net £
31 July	Aldo & Co	45	24.00	4.00	20.00
31 July	Hopley Brothers	46	36.00	6.00	30.00
31 July	Fernando's	47	25.20	4.20	21.00
31 July	Richmond Travel	48	38.40	6.40	32.00
	Totals		123.60	20.60	103.00

(a) What will be the entries in the general ledger? **(6 marks)**

Account name	Amount £	Debit ✓	Credit ✓
Discount allowed	103.00	✓	
VAT	20.60	✓	
Sales ledger control	123.60		✓

(b) What will be the entries in the subsidiary ledger? **(6 marks)**

Account name	Amount £	Debit ✓	Credit ✓
Abbs & Co	24.00		✓
Hoppley Brothers	36.00		✓
Fernando's	25.20		✓
Richmond travel	38.40		✓

TASK 1.7 **(12 marks)**

Roger's cash book is both a book of prime entry and part of the double entry bookkeeping system. The following transactions all took place on 31 December and have been entered in the debit side of the cash-book as shown below.

Cash-book – Debit side

Date 20XX	Details	Cash £	Bank £
31 Dec	Balance b/f	200	2,883
31 Dec	TUV Ltd		4,000

(a) What will be the entry in the sales ledger? **(3 marks)**

Sales ledger

Account name	Amount £	Debit ✓	Credit ✓
tuv Ltd	200		✓

(b) What will be the entry in the general ledger? **(3 marks)**

General ledger

Account name	Amount £	Debit ✓	Credit ✓
Sales ledger control Account	200		✓

The following transactions all took place on 31 December and have been entered in the credit side of the cash-book as shown below. No entries have yet been made in the ledgers.

Cash-book – Credit side

Date 20XX	Details	VAT £	Cash £	Bank £
31 Dec	Entertainment	32		192
31 Dec	Insurance			240

(c)   What will be the entries in the general ledger?   (6 marks)

General ledger

Account name	Amount £	Debit ✓	Credit ✓
Entertaiment	192	✓	
Insurance	240	✓	
V.At	32	✓	

TASK 1.8   (12 marks)

The following is a summary of transactions up to 31 December 20XX for Bella Pumpkin, a new credit customer.

£1,700 re invoice 1001 of 12 Dec
£2,350 re invoice 1004 of 21 Dec
£940 re credit note 101 of 21 Dec
£470 re invoice 1010 of 27 Dec
Cheque for £2,000 received 29 Dec

(a)   Enter the transactions into the sales ledger of Bella Pumpkin.   (5 marks)

(b)   Insert the balance carried down and the balance brought down together with date and details.   (2 marks)

Bella Pumpkin

Date 20XX	Details	Amount £	Date 20XX	Details	Amount £
12 Dec	Invoice 1001	1,700	21 Dic	Credit note 101	940
21 Dec	Invoice 1004	2,350	29 Dic	Cheque	2000
27 Dec	Invoice 1010	470	31 Dic	Balance d/d	1,580
		4,520			4,520
1 Jan	Balance b/d	1,580			

(c) Complete the statement of account below to be sent to Bella Pumpkin **(5 marks)**

<table>
<tr><td colspan="4" align="center">Rocky Ricardo
1 Rocky Way
Middleton, M42 5TU</td></tr>
<tr><td colspan="2">**To:** Bella Pumpkin</td><td colspan="2">**Date:** 31 Dec 20XX</td></tr>
<tr><td>**Date 20XX**</td><td>**Details**</td><td>**Transaction amount £**</td><td>**Outstanding amount £**</td></tr>
<tr><td>12 Dic</td><td>Invoice 1001</td><td>1,700</td><td>1,700</td></tr>
<tr><td>21 Dic</td><td>Invoice 1004</td><td>2,350</td><td>4,050</td></tr>
<tr><td>21 Dic</td><td>Credit note 101</td><td>940</td><td>3,110</td></tr>
<tr><td>27 Dic</td><td>Invoice 1010</td><td>470</td><td>3,580</td></tr>
<tr><td>29 Dic</td><td>Cheque</td><td>2000</td><td>1,580</td></tr>
</table>

TASK 1.9 (12 marks)

Below is an extract of balances from an organisation's trial balance.

(a) Calculate and insert the total of each of the debit and credit columns of the partially prepared trial balance. **(2 marks)**

Account name	Debit £	Credit £
Motor vehicles	27,268	
Inventory	18,592	
Petty cash control	200	
Sales ledger control (SLCA)	169,037	
Purchases ledger control (PLCA)		46,086
VAT owing to tax authorities (HMRC)		53,376
Capital		19,364
Loan from bank		16,413
Sales		550,064
Purchases	265,153	
Wages	152,199	
Motor expenses	5,403	
Rent and rates	10,345	
Advertising	2,486	
Telephone	1,599	
Miscellaneous expenses	8,281	
Totals	660,563	685,303

Shown below are the three final balances to be transferred to the trial balance.

(b) **Transfer each balance to the debit or credit column of the trial balance extract below.**

(3 marks)

Account name	Amount £	Debit £	Credit £
Bank overdraft	12,333		✓
Sales returns	38,873	✓	
Discount received	1,800		✓

The trial balance should now balance meaning the totals of the debit and credit columns should agree.

(c) **Calculate the final total entered into the debit and credit columns of the trial balance.**

(1 mark)

£ 699,436

The trial balance for a different organisation is being prepared and balances have been provided from the accounting records.

(d) **You are required to identify whether these accounts appear in the trial balance and if so whether they would be transferred to the debit or credit column.** (6 marks)

Sales ledger

Account name	Account balance	Transfers to the trial balance in the DEBIT column	Transfers to the trial balance in the CREDIT column	Does not transfer to the trial balance
		✓	✓	✓
Ella Bella's	£548			✓
Tony's Toys	£1,167			✓

Purchases ledger

Account name	Account balance	Transfers to the trial balance in the DEBIT column	Transfers to the trial balance in the CREDIT column	Does not transfer to the trial balance
		✓	✓	✓
PL & Co	£781			✓
Storage Supplies	£910			✓

General ledger

Account name	Account balance	Transfers to the trial balance in the DEBIT column ✓	Transfers to the trial balance in the CREDIT column ✓	Does not transfer to the trial balance ✓
Purchases returns	£1,200	✓	✓	
Fixtures and fittings	£3,000	✓		

TASK 1.10 (12 marks)

(a) It is important to understand the difference between capital expenditure, revenue expenditure, capital income and revenue income.

Select one option in each instance below to show whether the item will be capital expenditure, revenue expenditure, capital income or revenue income. (6 marks)

Item	Capital expenditure	Revenue expenditure	Capital income	Revenue income
Purchase of computer equipment	✓			
Receipts from credit sales			✓ ✗	✓
Receipt from sale of motor vehicle (non-current asset)			✓ ✓ ✗	
Purchase of motor vehicle	✓			
Purchase of stationery		✓		
Payment of rent		✓		

(b) Show whether the following statements are true or false. (3 marks)

Assets less liabilities are equal to capital   ~~True~~ / False

The business and owner are two separate entities   ~~True~~ / False

A debit increases an item of income   True / ~~False~~

(c) Classify each of the following items as an asset or a liability. (3 marks)

Item	Asset or liability?
Computer equipment	*Select* ~~Asset~~ OR Liability
Petty cash	*Select* ~~Asset~~ OR Liability
Money owed to suppliers	*Select* Asset OR ~~Liability~~

Section 4

MOCK ASSESSMENT ANSWERS

TASK 1.1 (12 marks)

(a) **Complete the invoice below.** (4 marks)

Rocky Ricardo					
1 Rocky Way					
Middleton, M42 5TU					

VAT Registration No. 298 3827 04

Alpha Group
Alpha House
Warwick
WR11 5TB

Customer account code: ALP01

Delivery note number: 2132

Date: 1 Dec 20XX

Invoice No: 950

Quantity of cases	Product code	Total list price £	Net amount after discount £	VAT £	Gross £
200	A1	2,000	1,800	360	2,160

(b) **What will be the amounts entered into the sales day book after the invoice in (a) has been prepared?** (3 marks)

Sales day book					
Date 20XX	Details	Invoice No:	Total £	VAT £	Net £
1 Dec	Alpha Group	950	2,160	360	1,800

(c) **Which item has not been included in the payment?** (2 marks)

Purchase invoice 189

(d) (i) **What is the amount Alpha Group should pay if payment is made within 5 days?** (2 marks)

£594

(ii) **What is the amount Alpha Group should pay if payment is NOT made within 5 days?** (1 mark)

£600

TASK 1.2 (9 marks)

(a) Check the invoice against the purchase order and answer the following questions.

(4 marks)

Has the correct discount been applied?	N
How much should the trade discount amount to?	£100
What would be the VAT amount charged if the invoice was correct?	£180

(b) What will be the details and amounts entered into the day book? (5 marks)

Day book: Purchase day book					
Date 20XX	Details	Invoice No:	Total £	VAT £	Net £
10 Dec	Messi Brothers	1365	2,250	375	1,875

TASK 1.3 (9 marks)

(a) Calculate the amount to be paid to each supplier if the prompt payment discount is taken and show the date by which the supplier should receive the payment. (4 marks)

Supplier	£	Date by which the payment should be received by the supplier
Bridge Brothers	110.25	23rd October
Mitchells	128.79	24th October

(b) Place a tick next to the 3 items in the supplier statement which will not be included within the payment. (3 marks)

Xcess Stock Unit 7 Windy Industrial Estate Irvine, KA6 8HU To: Lewin & Co Date: 31 Dec 20XX			Not to be paid
Date 20XX	Details	Transaction amount £	
12 Dec	Invoice 1001	1,700	
13 Dec	Invoice 1003	1,500	✓
21 Dec	Invoice 1004	2,350	
21 Dec	Credit note 101	940	
22 Dec	Invoice 1005	450	✓
27 Dec	Invoice 1010	470	
28 Dec	Credit note 102	50	✓

(c)   **What will be the amount paid to Xcess Stock by Lewin & Co? (1 mark)**

£3,580

(d)   One of the accounts within the purchases ledger of Lewin & Co is for the credit supplier Minto Madness. A credit note for a prompt payment discount of £20 plus VAT has been received from Minto Madness. Before processing the credit note, the balance on the account of Minto Madness is £1,540.

What is the amount remaining on the account taking into consideration the credit note?

(1 mark)

£1,516

TASK 1.4 (15 marks)

(a)   **Enter the details from the two receipts and three cheque book stubs into the credit side of the cash-book shown below and total each column.** **(6 marks)**

Cash book – Credit side

Details	Cash	Bank	VAT	Payables	Cash purchases	Motor expenses
Balance b/f		11,450				
J Pumpkin	960		160		800	
B Row	240		40		200	
Lemon Ltd		100		100		
Remo Motor		240	40			200
Fencer		600		600		
Total	1,200	12,390	240	700	1,000	200

(b)   **Enter the above details into the debit side of the cash-book and total each column.**

(4 marks)

Cash book – Debit side

Details	Cash	Bank	Receivables
Balance b/f	1,850		
Jeff Jolly		127	127
Dolly Darton		310	310
Total	1,850	437	437

(c)   **Using your answers to (a) and (b) above, calculate the cash balance.** **(2 marks)**

£650

(d)   **Using your answers to (a) and (b) above, calculate the bank balance.** **(2 marks)**

£11,953

(e)   **Will the bank balance calculated in (d) above be a debit or credit balance?** **(1 mark)**

Credit

TASK 1.5 (15 marks)

(a) Calculate the VAT and net amounts of this petty cash payment to be recorded in the petty cash book. **(2 marks)**

VAT £	Net £
12.00	60.00

(b) Calculate the total of the office expense analysis column after taking into consideration the petty cash payment in (a). **(1 mark)**

£80.00

(c) After taking into consideration the transaction in (a) what will be the entry in the petty cash book to restore to the imprest level of £200. **(3 marks)**

Details	Amount £	Debit ✓	Credit ✓
Cash from bank	134.40	✓	

Details picklist: Amount, Balance b/d, Balance c/d, Cash from bank

(d) What is the entry made in the petty cash book to record the closing balance on 30th June? **(3 marks)**

Details	Amount £	Debit ✓	Credit ✓
Balance c/d	200.00		✓

(e) For each receipt identify the analysis column to be used for the payment and the amount of the transaction that should be recorded in the analysis column. **(6 marks)**

Petty cash receipt	Analysis column	Amount £
Printing Partners	Office expenses	41.15
Annan Motor Supplies	Motor expenses	14.50
Your Local Convenience	Cleaning expenses	5.60

TASK 1.6 (12 marks)

(a) What will be the entries in the general ledger? **(6 marks)**

Account name	Amount £	Debit ✓	Credit ✓
Sales ledger control	123.60		✓
VAT	20.60	✓	
Discounts allowed	103.00	✓	

(b) **What will be the entries in the subsidiary ledger?** (6 marks)

Account name	Amount £	Debit ✓	Credit ✓
Aldo & Co	24.00		✓
Hopley Brothers	36.00		✓
Fernando's	25.20		✓
Richmond Travel	38.40		✓

TASK 1.7 (12 marks)

(a) **What will be the entry in the sales ledger?** (3 marks)

Sales ledger

Account name	Amount £	Debit ✓	Credit ✓
TUV Ltd	4,000		✓

(b) **What will be the entry in the general ledger?** (3 marks)

General ledger

Account name	Amount £	Debit ✓	Credit ✓
Sales ledger control	4,000		✓

(c) **What will be the entries in the general ledger?** (6 marks)

General ledger

Account name	Amount £	Debit ✓	Credit ✓
Entertainment	160	✓	
VAT	32	✓	
Insurance	240	✓	

TASK 1.8 (12 marks)

(a) – (b)

Bella Pumpkin

Date 20XX	Details	Amount £	Date 20XX	Details	Amount £
12 Dec	Invoice 1001	1,700	21 Dec	Credit note 101	940
21 Dec	Invoice 1004	2,350	29 Dec	Cheque rec'd	2,000
27 Dec	Invoice 1010	470	31 Dec	Balance c/d	1,580
		4,520			**4,520**
20XY 1 Jan	Balance b/d	1,580			

(c)　Complete the statement of account below to be sent to Bella Pumpkin　(5 marks)

Rocky Ricardo
1 Rocky Way
Middleton, M42 5TU

To: Bella Pumpkin　　　　　　　　　　　　　　　　**Date:** 31 Dec 20XX

Date 20XX	Details	Transaction amount £	Outstanding amount £
12 Dec	Invoice 1001	1,700	1,700
21 Dec	Invoice 1004	2,350	4,050
21 Dec	Credit note 101	940	3,110
27 Dec	Invoice 1010	470	3,580
29 Dec	Cheque	2,000	1,580

TASK 1.9 (12 marks)

(a) Calculate and insert the total of each of the debit and credit columns of the partially prepared trial balance. (2 marks)

Account name	Debit £	Credit £
Motor vehicles	27,268	
Inventory	18,592	
Petty cash control	200	
Sales ledger control (SLCA)	169,037	
Purchases ledger control (PLCA)		46,086
VAT owing to tax authorities (HMRC)		53,376
Capital		19,364
Loan from bank		16,413
Sales		550,064
Purchases	265,153	
Wages	152,199	
Motor expenses	5,403	
Rent and rates	10,345	
Advertising	2,486	
Telephone	1,599	
Miscellaneous expenses	8,281	
Totals	**660,563**	**685,303**

(b) Transfer each balance to the debit or credit column of the trial balance extract below. (3 marks)

Account name	Amount £	Debit £	Credit £
Bank overdraft	12,333		12,333
Sales returns	38,873	38,873	
Discount received	1,800		1,800

(c) Calculate the final total entered into the debit and credit columns of the trial balance. (1 mark)

£699,436

(d) You are required to identify whether these accounts appear in the trial balance and if so whether they would be transferred to the debit or credit column. **(6 marks)**

Sales ledger

Account name	Account balance	Transfers to the trial balance in the DEBIT column ✓	Transfers to the trial balance in the CREDIT column ✓	Does not transfer to the trial balance ✓
Ella Bella's	£548			✓
Tony's Toys	£1,167			✓

Purchases ledger

Account name	Account balance	Transfers to the trial balance in the DEBIT column ✓	Transfers to the trial balance in the CREDIT column ✓	Does not transfer to the trial balance ✓
PL & Co	£781			✓
Storage Supplies	£910			✓

General ledger

Account name	Account balance	Transfers to the trial balance in the DEBIT column ✓	Transfers to the trial balance in the CREDIT column ✓	Does not transfer to the trial balance ✓
Purchases returns	£1,200		✓	
Fixtures and fittings	£3,000	✓		

TASK 1.10 (12 marks)

(a) Select one option in each instance below to show whether the item will be capital expenditure, revenue expenditure, capital income or revenue income. (6 marks)

Item	Capital expenditure	Revenue expenditure	Capital income	Revenue income
Purchase of computer equipment	✓			
Receipts from credit sales				✓
Receipt from sale of motor vehicle (non-current asset)			✓	
Purchase of motor vehicle	✓			
Purchase of stationery		✓		
Payment of rent		✓		

(b) Show whether the following statements are true or false. (3 marks)

Assets less liabilities are equal to capital	True
The business and owner are two separate entities	True
A debit increases an item of income	False

(c) Classify each of the following items as an asset or a liability. (3 marks)

Item	Asset or liability?
Computer equipment	Asset
Petty cash	Asset
Money owed to suppliers	Liability

TASK 1.10